PUFFIN PLUS
From Schoolboy to Sup

There are many ways of becoming a professional footballer. Some young players become attached to a club when they are still at school; others – like England international Steve Coppell – have spent three years at university and then managed to succeed in the game.

Guardian football correspondent Patrick Barclay here describes the careers of a number of stars – including Steve Coppell, Micky Phelan of Burnley and Sammy Lee – and shows just how they made it to the top. And in one particularly fine chapter he hears what it was like for young Tony Cottee the day he made his debut for West Ham at the age of seventeen.

Not that soccer is all glamour and success. Many schoolboy stars don't make the step smoothly into the professional game, and inevitably they endure a lot of disappointment and heartache along the way. It's their story too which Patrick Barclay tells.

From Schoolboy to Superstar is essential reading for any youngster who thinks he might want to be a professional footballer. It shows just how he can set about it. But beyond that, anyone interested in sport will find the book a fascinating account of how the game operates.

Patrick Barclay

FROM SCHOOLBOY
TO SUPERSTAR

PUFFIN BOOKS

Puffin Books, Penguin Books Ltd, Harmondsworth, Middlesex, England
Penguin Books, 40 West 23rd Street, New York, New York 10010, U.S.A.
Penguin Books Australia Ltd, Ringwood, Victoria, Australia
Penguin Books Canada Ltd, 2801 John Street, Markham, Ontario, Canada L3R 1B4
Penguin Books (N.Z.) Ltd, 182–190 Wairau Road, Auckland 10, New Zealand

First published 1983

Copyright © Patrick Barclay, 1983
All rights reserved

Made and printed in Great Britain by
Cox & Wyman Ltd, Reading
Filmset in Monophoto Photina by Northumberland Press Ltd, Gateshead

Except in the United States of America, this book is sold subject
to the condition that it shall not, by way of trade or otherwise, be lent,
re-sold, hired out, or otherwise circulated without the
publisher's prior consent in any form of binding or cover other than
that in which it is published and without a similar condition
including this condition being imposed on the subsequent purchaser

For Chris

INTRODUCTION

The absence of a well-constructed development programme for football during the school years and beyond has caused a gradual decline in the standard of play within the United Kingdom. From the end of the First World War until the 1950s, football, its techniques and its skills, were learned from long hours of practice in the back streets and on the wastelands of our urban areas – and talent was abundant. However, the dramatic improvement in social welfare within the United Kingdom in the 1950s created a different attitude towards sport and leisure activities. Young people now have infinitely more opportunities to follow all kinds of leisure activities.

The result is that football skills are no longer practised, mastered and used in the back streets and alleyways in the way they once were. The small-sided games that could last all day and were the informal tests of skill now rarely occur and no substitute for them has emerged.

These 'practice/play' periods were vital in developing young players' skills as they allowed a great deal of 'trial and error' without fear of failure. Thus, skills could be modified and perfected away from the pressures of organized competition.

Schools' football has given little thought to the acquisition of football skill or the development of football talent in this new situation. Instead, time and effort has been spent in creating a huge framework of competitive match-play in which, from a very early age, youngsters are ruthlessly 'examined' without receiving sufficient information on how to perform. Practice and experimentation have been sacrificed. The 'magic' formula that produced so many stars in the past has been exchanged for a pressurized system of development that produces an abundance of low-skilled, stereotyped competitors.

Whilst travelling throughout the United Kingdom I find many good teachers, parents and coaches who are dissatisfied with the present misdirected approach. This disenchantment with the game must be rechannelled into a positive movement towards a better system of player development. We cannot turn the clock back to a time when players developed their skills more naturally, but we should be able to learn from the past and employ a more intelligent approach to the development of football talent in the future. Perhaps some of the following suggestions could be implemented:

1. A national football development programme should be devised.
2. More emphasis should be given to the small-sided game throughout the school system.
3. Schools should allow more contact with professional coaches.
4. Schools of excellence should be set up so that football talent can be nurtured in the same way that other subjects are given specialized teaching.

The game's leaders at all levels must show a more visionary and courageous approach to football skill development. By clinging to the crumbling remnants of a system that does not and cannot produce high quality players, we will continue to deny this wonderful game of Association Football the number of stars and superstars it demands and deserves.

JOHN CARTWRIGHT, former coach of the England Youth Squad

May 1983

FROM SCHOOLBOY TO SUPERSTAR

CHAPTER ONE

Steve Coppell grew up like thousands of other boys in Liverpool – with a ball at his feet. It was during the Sixties, the first Beatles era, but for young Steve the most appealing rhythm was not that of the exciting new sound. It was the familiar, monotonous thud, thud, thud of his ball hitting a wall. He was learning the skills that were to help him become a star with Manchester United and England. But he did not know it then. To Steve and all the other boys football was fun, fantasy even, and it was not until several years later that he was invited to train with Tranmere Rovers and the game began to change his life.

The first morning at Tranmere taught him a swift, sudden lesson he has never forgotten. They played a five-a-side game, and Steve made a couple of bad passes. Just a couple. Some days it happens that way, as every schoolboy footballer knows, so Steve was surprised when he was immediately pulled aside by Johnny King, the Tranmere coach. 'Listen,' said King, 'you aren't playing football for enjoyment now.' He jabbed a thumb in the direction of the other young players. 'These lads depend on it for a living. You'd better realize that straight away.'

From that stinging moment Steve Coppell, the young man with dreams in his head, became Steve Coppell, the professional. His attitude changed for ever. He became dedicated. And every boy at school today who wants to make a living from the world's greatest game will have to do the same.

He too will have to forsake his dreams for hard reality. He will have to work, ration his visits to the disco, perhaps even go on a permanent diet. He will have to take criticism in his stride and be single-minded. Not everyone will strike out for success the hard way, as Steve did in combining his blossoming football career with studies at university, but there will be difficult choices for all – and in the end very few will reach base camp, let alone the summit.

Because the chances of success are so slim, there is no disgrace in failure. Later in this book you will read the story of Tony Burke, a young man with skill in abundance who dropped out of the professional ranks before his 18th birthday. After meeting him you may not consider the word 'failure' appropriate. You may, in fact, learn as much from meeting Tony as you will from Steve Coppell, Sammy Lee, Tony Cottee, Dennis Tueart, Mick Phelan and such respected off-the-field judges as Bobby Robson and Tom Saunders. But first let's find out what made Steve Coppell an England star.

The story begins with disappointment. When Steve was 15, small but obviously talented, he was told by his headmaster in Liverpool that trials with the city's schoolboys were forbidden. Steve was at Quarry Bank, the same school as the former Everton and England centre-forward Joe Royle, now manager of Oldham Athletic. Joe had missed a lot of school because of football and eventually left before taking O-levels. The headmaster said it would never happen again. 'It broke my heart,' Steve recalls. He was at the age when promising players were being picked for representative teams and becoming associated with clubs. 'My dream was to be a footballer and I thought the only way was to be spotted young and become an apprentice with a club. I remember thinking "I'll never be a footballer now."'

Looking back, however, Steve realizes that the headmaster's decision did him a favour. He swallowed his disappointment and concentrated on studying for exams. He passed O-levels, then A-levels, and in between started to grow – a more important factor than bigger youths may realize. Steve didn't measure 5 foot until he was 17, before shooting to his present height of 5 foot 7 inches in a matter of months, and he disputes the old saying 'if you're good enough you're big enough' with memories of frustrating combat against the towering 6-footers he often faced. He would still have been growing towards the end of an apprenticeship period, and might have become one of the disappointed majority who are released.

In the years following he was to see at Old Trafford how unhappy the apprentice's lot can be. 'You can be a good lad and still be told at 17 or 18 that you're not going to make it, maybe on the opinion of just one person. It's as well to be prepared. I have seen arrogant apprentices who think they have arrived because they have been taken on by a big club. They just don't realize that they are struggling for survival.'

At 17 Steve had abandoned all hope of becoming a professional footballer. Little did he know that the door was far from closed. He was still enjoying his game, playing for the school on a Saturday morning and Norris Green Boys' Club in the afternoon. Norris Green had a good side and it was there that Steve was spotted by a scout, Eddie Edwards, who asked him along to Tranmere. At first Steve, still feeling a shade disillusioned about his prospects, told Edwards he was concentrating on A-levels. But Edwards persisted and eventually Steve went for a trial.

What happened on that day, he says, is a perfect illustration that football is a matter of other people's opinions. He says: 'The day I had my trial I was playing alongside the lad I played with at the boys' club. I scored three goals, but it was all down to the big fellow knocking them off. I just put the goals in, more or less. At the end they asked me to come back for training and they didn't ask the big fellow. That seemed very unfair to me. He's an architect now.'

After finishing A-levels, Steve, then 18, went straight into pre-season training with Tranmere, and Johnny King soon brought home to him that he was in a different world where football and flippancy did not mix. One day's experience gave him a professional attitude. Yet even then Steve had a level-headed approach to his future. He thought going to university would still provide a more practical way of earning a living than football, certainly in the longer term. So he went to Liverpool University and combined his studies with professional football.

He was fortunate to receive advice on how to do this. Another part-timer in the Tranmere team, Mark Palios, was already at Manchester University and helped him to work out a training schedule. 'When I was tired of studying I went to football,' says Steve, 'and when I was tired of football I studied.' Later he was also grateful for the understanding of Tommy Docherty, then United's manager, who advised him to stay on at university, training alone, apart from one morning a week with the Old Trafford squad.

What did not figure in his schedule was a social life. This may surprise you, since university is supposed to be a place for socializing as well as studying, but even after Steve had been transferred to United and had become an established member of one of Europe's most glamorous teams, he did not attend a single function. His first disco came in his third year, by which time he was 21. He says he didn't miss the social life – because he didn't know what he was missing!

Dedication also meant organizing his own training, even after he had moved from Tranmere to United. From the start Steve made this assessment: 'I'm basically a fit fellow, so I don't need much fitness training. I'm going to work with the ball.' He practised control by hitting it against a wall for one and a half hours at a time. That was his training every day. It may sound a lonely existence, but then it's often the work players put in on their own that helps them to the top. After all, squad training sessions, whether with Tranmere, Manchester United, or even England, cannot possibly cater for every individual need. The most successful players are often those who stay behind to practise a skill. They might even make a habit of studying video recordings of matches they played in, seeking to spot weaknesses that can be put right. They are the ones with that special drive and ambition to reach the top, and Steve points to Kevin Keegan as the outstanding example.

Keegan used to work extremely hard during organized training with England, then stay behind for shooting and heading practice. And that was the England captain, a man whose footballing exploits had already earned a lifetime's prosperity for his family and himself. At United it's a similar story today with Frank Stapleton, who is almost always out on the training field the longest.

To become a successful footballer often requires considerable mental discipline. It is not simply a question of making sure you do enough training. You might also have to watch what, or how much, you eat and drink. Some players such as Sammy Lee, whom we will meet later, don't worry about the food intake too much, but Steve is a firm believer in keeping the brakes on. He says: 'I often feel, oh hell, why can't I have a piece of cheesecake? But I know that if I have something sweet like a biscuit I'll eat a load of them. Most players are the same. Ray Wilkins, for example, has got the strongest willpower I have ever seen as regards eating. If he ate a normal diet he'd put on three-quarters of a stone and he knows it. You have to get used to being at an artificial weight, like a jockey. If you don't you can get too heavy and drift out of the game. Ray Kennedy and Joe Corrigan are good examples of people who were sensible enough to realize that, just in time to save their careers.'

The difference between the professional and the amateur can be seen on any public park. People have come up to Steve and told him: 'We've got a lad playing for our pub team on a Saturday who could have been a professional. He's brilliant.' Sometimes Steve has made a point of seeing the player and, as often as not, he is very talented indeed. But he clearly spends too much time in the pub. In other typical cases he might have been attached to a club as a youngster but did not like the training, or the trainer. 'So many say that,' says Steve. His brother, a good keen amateur, has played with some exceptionally talented people who Steve believes could probably survive in the First Division were it not for the fact that they were not prepared to put up with the disadvantages.

It's beginning to sound as if little more than hard work and determination took Steve to fame and the World Cup. That is not, of course, the whole story. The main reason for his success is his innate ability, nurtured by a football-mad childhood in which he played every day, winter and summer, along with just about every other kid in the neighbourhood. At that time there were none of the sophisticated toys and electronic games that the more fortunate children have today. Steve cannot even remember watching television until he was 13. There is another important difference today, says Steve, with young footballers neglecting street or park games in favour of official, organized coaching courses. 'It's a pity,' he says, 'because a lot of every player's skill or flair can only be developed when he is very young. I find it sad driving round the area where I grew up and seldom seeing a street game.'

In his formative years Steve received just the right amount

of gentle guidance from his father, a keen football fan, who took him to matches at Liverpool. He also went to watch Steve play, would pass on a few tips, but never tried to take control of his training. 'That was important,' says Steve, 'I have been able to develop in my own way.' He is the first to admit, however, that he received help along the road to success. Modestly, he says luck played a big part, giving as an example Tranmere's decision to take him on instead of the big lad who laid on his three goals in the trial. He is also grateful for the faith showed by Ron Yeats, Tranmere's manager at the time of his promotion to the first team as a teenager, and to the guidance of Tommy Docherty and Tommy Cavanagh when he went to Old Trafford. 'But,' he says, 'as far as training is concerned, I have taken care to be master of my own destiny.' That obviously suited Steve. It would not suit everybody. But, as we are to discover, the road to success can be hard and lonely and self-reliance is a priceless asset.

CHAPTER TWO

Football is, to a large extent, something you can teach yourself. And this is one of the game's great strengths. Learning it does not require the best facilities, nor the most expensive equipment. Indeed some people would say that these can be a disadvantage. Many professionals believe that youngsters are coming through with less skill than before, and such experienced observers as Tom Saunders, youth development officer at Liverpool, put this down to the decline of good, old-fashioned, street football. The way towns and cities are planned these days, not to mention the increase in traffic, has made these games less practical, less safe, and less popular. In the 1930s, Tom recalls, he used to run errands with a tennis ball at his feet, controlling it all the way. He spent every spare moment of his young life playing football of one sort or another. The games were always competitive, instilling the vital skills of control and quick thinking. When you played four boys against five in the narrow, confined spaces of the cobbled streets and back alleys, you simply had to learn.

Though ways of life have changed over the years, many of today's top players developed their skills the same way. Steve Coppell's boyhood experiences, for instance, are echoed by the and former England forward Dennis Tueart, who was also brought up in a city on a staple diet of football. Dennis lived in Walker, a district of Newcastle upon Tyne that lies in the shadow of the shipyards where his father worked. The type of football he and his friends played was called 'gates' or 'doors' because there was a back lane running behind the rows of houses and everybody had a door, which served as his goal. There would be four or five boys playing at a time and, with space restricted, each player was in constant touch with the ball. You had to solve your own problems, and not only with the ball either.

Footwear was a problem because, as Dennis recalls, 'Like most kids of my age I had a pair of shoes for school and a pair for Sundays. There was no way I had a pair for playing football in the streets. So I got a worn-out pair of my father's working shoes, when he was finished with them, and cut out soles from a piece of linoleum and fixed them to the bottoms. They were a few sizes too big, but even that helped because it made control more difficult. I had to try harder. Nowadays a lot of the kids are dressed up to the nines, with training shoes and so on, but the best tracksuits and footwear don't make them better players.'

Dennis, like Steve, notices significant changes when he goes back today to the scene of his boyhood. In his part of Walker, there were four large blocks of flats, backing on to each other, and in the middle was an area known as 'the green', where boys would play football. The grass was always worn away, so that apart from a few patches it was 'green' in name alone. Now, Dennis has noticed, that square of grass is in perfect condition. 'It's lovely,' he says, 'and I think that's indicative. There are still plenty of kids living around the flats, you can see them playing, but they are not playing football on the green. It is hardly surprising that skilful schoolboy players are not coming through in the same numbers as they used to.'

The changing picture saddens Bobby Robson, whose success during thirteen years as manager of Ipswich Town, between 1969 and his move to the England job, was built partly on developing schoolboys into excellent professionals. Like Dennis, Bobby is from the footballing stronghold of the north-east of England and he, too, is concerned about falling standards of school technique. We have lost the backstreet footballers, he says, because we have lost the back streets. But he doesn't see why boys themselves shouldn't put the matter right, as the successful ones will always do, by practising. He says, 'As a kid I would play with a tin can or a tennis ball. But it was always football. Now they play all sorts of sports in the schools rather than specializing. Today, when I see the standard of some of our schoolboys I have to say to them – go back to school and play, play, play, as much as you can, wherever you can. You won't learn the game by watching television, or climbing trees. And, although you should take every chance you can get to go on coaching courses, you won't become a player that way either. The most important thing is to play. If the back streets are not there any more, find somewhere else, the school grounds, maybe, but play, play, play.'

At Ipswich Bobby always made a point of supervising the schoolboy trials at the club's training ground. These lasted for several days at a time. A selected forty would come, fifteen-year-olds from all over Britain, recommended by Ipswich scouts. And despite his pessimism about levels of technique, he would often see half a dozen with distinct possibilities of being made into professional footballers. The boys come down at Christmas, Easter and half-term to be assessed by the manager and coaching staff. If they find four or five with the potential of, say, an Alan Brazil, they will feel they have done well.

The qualities Bobby and the other managers look for are many. They range from the technical skills such as control, passing and heading, through the athletic attributes of speed, stamina, jumping ability and so on, to those very important matters of enthusiasm and character that all professionals stress. In all his time at Ipswich, Bobby can remember only one young player who had everything – and that was Kevin Beattie. 'Beattie was one in a lifetime. He had all the skills and passing ability and when you tried to tackle him it was like hitting a tank!'

Bobby looks for a dozen things in a player. Beattie may have had them all, but a much less naturally endowed player could still have a chance of being signed as apprentice if the club had a hunch about his potential. Alan Brazil, for instance, had only two obvious assets when he came down from Scotland – strength, and a good left foot. 'In all honesty,' says Bobby, 'that was about all. He couldn't head a ball, he was short of control, wasn't much of a dribbler. But you just knew that if you put him in a clear position with the goal in front of him he might score. We thought he was worth being patient with, and built up all the other things gradually. He was a listener, a good pupil, and in six years he became a top-class international player.'

The associate schoolboy stage was Brazil's first step on the road to becoming a professional. His was the route taken by those boys who are spotted by the scouts. Scouts can be former professionals but as often as not they are local teachers, and Tom Saunders maintains that this country's talent-spotting network is the envy of the world. But as the man in charge of developing youngsters for Liverpool, whose first-team standards are so demanding, he stresses that being spotted is only the beginning of a long, often heartbreaking process for the boy and his parents. 'As soon as someone becomes the subject of interest,' he says, 'the people from clubs come knocking on his door and as often as not it's the boy's mother and father, however sensible they may be, who get carried away. You tell them to bide their time, to get him educated, but they are up in the air and it's a hell of a job to pull them down again. What they do not realize is that anything that looks remotely like a prospective footballer is in demand. The vast majority of them will not make it. I actually did a survey when I was involved with the England schoolboys – the cream, who are able to pick and choose which club they will go to – and the truth was that 65 per cent of them were not employed in football at the age of 18. A lot of them may have suffered from being kidded and letting their education take second place.'

Competition among the clubs for schoolboys can be a cut-throat business. Liverpool, for instance, are strong believers that boys should become associated with their local clubs, but a youngster in demand, and his parents, can have pressure put on them by clubs from further afield. It is not unknown for clubs to promise a parent that his son will be signed as an apprentice when he reaches 16, which is the next step, or even that he will be given a professional contract later – with such-and-such a salary and a handsome signing-on fee.

Dishonesty does creep in, for despite the F.A. rules forbidding such payments it is a fact that parents have been offered inducements – visits to hotels, meals, jobs as scouts, or even large sums of money. One particularly outstanding youngster now with a northern club was said to have earned his parents a 'transfer fee' of £16,000 when he signed as an apprentice a few years ago. Liverpool, says Tom, are content to go about things in a more ethical way and adds: 'We can look people in the eye, show them our training facilities, and if at the end of the day they choose to go else-where we say, "Sorry, we wish you the very best of luck."'

Simply getting a boy's name on a form, without ready access to him, surely defeats the object of association. If he goes to a club from outside his area, he cannot receive the regular training and assessment, two nights a week, that take place at Liverpool. Ipswich might argue that their record in developing young players indicates the opposite. Nevertheless Tom maintains that the more discerning parent will usually send his son to be trained locally. 'The age 14 to 16,' he says, 'is a critical period, when the boy may have to cope with outside pressures if he is particularly successful as a young player. Lots of people will want to claim credit for his success. I found it with the England schoolboys – one teacher would carry the boy's bag, another would carry his boots. He's playing at big grounds, staying in big hotels. He's living in a fool's paradise.'

The associate schoolboy is well advised, then, to keep his feet firmly on the ground. Part of Tom's job, as he sees it, is to make sure that they do, while Liverpool assess them. The club have between twenty and twenty-five boys at a time, some of whom find the work too hard and drop out. The boys go to the club's well-equipped training ground at Melwood two nights a week, from quarter to six to half past seven. At Liverpool all the coaches like to be involved, which means that Ronnie Moran, the chief coach, when he has finished working with Kenny Dalglish, Ian Rush, Graeme Souness, Phil Neal, and the others, takes an interest in the boy. So does Roy Evans, the man in charge of Liverpool's highly successful reserve side. They and the others find it relaxing as well as satisfying to work with youngsters. Like Bobby Robson, they realize where the game's future lies. During these sessions at Melwood there's not too much emphasis on formal coaching. Generally the boys play small-sided team games for, as Tom says: 'They're encouraged to find the answers to problems themselves. It's the way we teach lads at Liverpool, right up to first-team level. You won't find Liverpool players looking over to the bench during a match, asking what position they should be taking up or who they should be marking. We believe in players having a sense of responsibility.'

During these small-sided games the Liverpool staff will be assessing each boy's character as well as his ability. 'If he's selfish,' says Tom, 'it will show in his play. If his head drops when everything is not going his way, it will show. If he is not all that determined to win, it will show. If his heart is not too big, that will show – and these, to us, are vital points. We will note them.' The associate schoolboy period is, in fact, principally a time for the club to make an assessment. They believe that the vital attribute of 'character', the will to win, is something that comes from a boy's background and cannot be instilled, no matter how much coaching he is given. Tom relates a story of the time he was called out to Israel to coach and was instructed, 'All we want you to do is put the Englishman's aggression into the Israeli footballer.' He replied, 'In that case it is impossible.' And the job was promptly abandoned! 'It would have been dishonest,' he says, 'to pretend that I could put something into people whose environment had made them a different way.'

As Tom readily admits, professional football is a hard world, ruthless at times, and it's as well to be prepared. He never takes on a boy without first telling the parents or guardians to prepare him for an alternative job. He might not be good enough for football, and should be able to develop as a person without feeling he has to succeed in the game at all costs. The portrayal of football as a glamorous occupation, like that of a pop star, Tom regrets, but he would have to admit that these schoolboy dreams are part of the reason young people want to be players in the first place. Indeed every young footballer would do well to take as his text the words of Rudyard Kipling in the poem 'If ...' – 'If you can dream, and not make dreams your master ...' With such an attitude he would have made an excellent youth development officer for a Football League club!

Three months before his sixteenth birthday, every associate schoolboy is told whether the club thinks he has a chance of making a living out of the game. If the answer is 'Yes' he will be offered an apprenticeship. As Steve Coppell has said, the apprentice's life is certainly not a glamorous one, nor by any means the exclusive method of getting into the professional ranks, but it is an important step. We will find out soon what it's like to be taken on – and to be shown the door by people like Tom, who says: 'It's not a part of the job I enjoy and I enjoy it even less now that jobs outside football have become more scarce.'

This, of course, underlines his point that education is paramount. And every year, when he gets together the parents of the eight or ten sixteen-year-olds who are being taken on as apprentices, he tells them: 'If your lad has the slightest academic bent, keep him at school as long as possible.' He says this in the certain knowledge that, if they have got what professional clubs are looking for, they will still have it in a few years' time even if they go to university like Steve Coppell or the former Liverpool players Brian Hall and Steve Heighway. Sometimes it's more difficult to get this over to the parents, who may have been bombarded with what Tom calls 'sales talk' from other clubs, than to the boys themselves. He is adamant though, because he has seen so many apprentices who are rejected at 18 without any qualifications for life.

Education is available, of course, to all apprentices and there is excellent advice to be had from Bob Kerry, who works from the Professional Footballers' Association offices in Manchester. But as Tom says: 'You can lead a horse to water, but you cannot make it drink. We have arranged all sorts of courses for lads, after finding out their strengths and weaknesses, but in the end many of them just aren't interested. They are wasting the colleges' time, and we have had to tell the parents so.' They could all take a lesson from Kipling.

CHAPTER THREE

Tom Saunders is well aware of what some of his competitors say about Liverpool. It's no good going there, they tell talented youngsters, because you won't get a chance to break through into the first team. And if you look at the side which took Liverpool to two successive championships you will see that they have a point. Every player but two had been brought to Anfield from another club. One of those exceptions was Phil Thompson, and even he was not a first choice for part of the 1981/2 season. The other, the only home-grown talent to play throughout the two campaigns, was Sammy Lee.

So what makes Sammy special? Obviously he is a very talented player, but character is important, too, and on meeting him the first thing that strikes you is an impressive sense of responsibility. Liverpool, as Tom pointed out, like players to work out the answers to problems for themselves, and Sammy's personality is ideally suited to this. He is a modest, polite young man. Like Ian Callaghan, his predecessor in the Liverpool midfield, Sammy's good nature shows on the field, where he seldom resorts to fouling an opponent. But like Callaghan he combines sportsmanship with a dedication to being successful in the game that no one could question. He works hard and is constantly, unselfishly involved in the action during every match he plays. Those were the qualities that most attracted Tom when he saw Sammy in a county F.A. Cup Final at Melwood eight years ago. Indeed Sammy's progress since the day he signed for Liverpool at 16 is a perfect illustration of why, from time immemorial, people in the professional game have stressed that young players must 'keep their feet on the ground' to fulfil their potential.

Though in his schoolboy days Sammy shared the familiar dreams of stardom, he did not think he was good enough to be a professional footballer. In fact he almost had to be forced into the game by the disappointment of failing seven O-levels out of nine. He had concentrated on his studies at St Francis Xavier College in Woolton with the intention of taking A-levels and eventually becoming a surveyor. 'I knew Liverpool were interested in me,' he says, 'but I wanted to stay at school until 18 on the basis that, if the club thought I was good enough, they would still want me then. I didn't think I should risk being thrown on the scrapheap at 18, as so many lads are, without qualifications. But two O-levels out of nine was, well, grim – so I had to be a footballer!'

He might have ended up with Everton, where he trained as a fourteen-year-old, but the school disapproved at that time and it was not until he was 16, having missed out on the chance of being an associate schoolboy, that he went instead to Liverpool. Tom spotted him on the club's training ground, where he played for his Sunday League team. 'I think Everton thought I would go back to them when I finished school,' he says, 'and Coventry came in too. But I was impressed with Liverpool because Tom Saunders was so honest and straightforward with me. He told me "It's all down to yourself." He wasn't making promises he couldn't keep. That impressed me.'

Thus Sammy became a Liverpool apprentice, which meant arriving at Anfield at nine o'clock each morning to set out the kit and perform other tasks such as making sure the baths were clean. It also meant cleaning the boots of a more senior player. In Sammy's case the player was Kevin Kewley, a striker who made just one appearance as a substitute before being transferred to Dallas Tornado, the now defunct North American Soccer League club. 'That was my claim to fame at the time,' says Sammy. 'Actually Kevin was a good player, very underestimated.' At 17 Sammy was made a full professional. He was relieved of the more menial jobs and did not have to arrive in the morning until ten o'clock, which remains the case now that he is in the first team.

Liverpool's players are taken by coach every day from Anfield to Melwood, where they train for two hours before returning for lunch and a rest in the players' lounge at the ground. The afternoons are free, though as Sammy says, 'I feel as if I do a hard day's work. I reckon I do as much in two hours at Melwood as most people do in eight at a normal job.' There is, says Sammy, very little coaching of the text-book kind. The coaches look for 'bad habits' and try to correct them, but above all the players are encouraged to express themselves within the team framework. 'This club relies on experience and there's enough of that among the coaching staff to last any player a lifetime. They let you know about your faults. With me, for instance, I don't use my left foot and also I had a tendency to chip a lot, leaning back, rather than getting over the top of the ball. These are bad habits.' But significantly he finds it difficult to single out the member of staff who has been most influential on his career. 'I was under Roy Evans for a few years and he was certainly a big influence, but Bob Paisley, Joe Fagan, Ronnie Moran, Tom Saunders ... they have all been equally helpful because at this club everybody speaks to everybody else and helps each other out. It's the good thing about Liverpool.'

Apart from the coaching staff Sammy has also taken a few football lessons from his parents, who even today are quick to point out parts of his game that need attention

– above all that little matter of the neglected left foot. They took a keen interest in his progress as a schoolboy and still watch all Liverpool's home matches, though the demands of the family butcher's shop mean that they cannot travel to away fixtures. It is a happy, close-knit family, reflected in the sight of an England Under 21 captain delivering meat in his father's van when training is over, but Sammy says the decision to go to Liverpool was his alone. 'I owe my parents an awful lot for what they have done for my career,' he says, 'but nobody told me to go to Liverpool. You have to stand or fall by your own decisions.'

He now lives in a flat where as often as not his choice of relaxation is to select something from his collection of old films and put it on the video player. Among his favourites are Basil Rathbone (as Sherlock Holmes), Humphrey Bogart, and above all James Cagney – 'He's brilliant, so exuberant'. The opportunity is there to go out and over-indulge in pastimes less compatible with being an athlete, but Sammy puts his career first. As he says: 'The Sunday League sides are full of skilful players who like to drink and have a good time. Of course, I've been tempted in that direction, but the way I look at it is: if you work hard and get to the top, the good times will come later. You get a lot of good times in football and I'd certainly rather wait for a good time in football than have a good time now and be out of work. The restrictions you have to put up with are not too bad, except maybe on Christmas night when I feel specially sorry for the lads who have families. But you simply have to cut out most of the social life. If you didn't it would show in your play.'

Surprisingly Sammy does not observe a special diet in the way Steve Coppell and Ray Wilkins find necessary. 'I eat a lot,' he says, 'and I eat what I want. I get called "Porky" or "Fatty" by the other players at Liverpool but as long as

I can get round the field on a Saturday that's all I'm worried about. I feel comfortable. Nobody's ever hinted that I might go on a diet, and maybe that's part of the reason for Liverpool's success – self-discipline. They treat you like an adult and leave the way you live to your own common sense. Mind you, if the way you live starts to affect your performance you're out, and that's it!'

Liverpool, says Sammy, are at the top because people there *want* to be at the top. But nothing is taken for granted. The most thrilling period of his career was in 1980, when he broke into the first team. Since then he has made nearly 200 appearances, yet he says: 'I don't look upon myself as a regular in the team. Not here. I won't be a regular until I have played 500 games. That's not being pessimistic. That's the way it is.'

Regular or not, Sammy has had to cope in the last couple of years with the fact that his face is known by the public. Being noticed in the street has its good points and bad points, he says, and the disadvantages include having to put up with people whose manners clearly do not match his own. There are Liverpool supporters, for instance, who do not think he should be in the team and feel a need to tell him so. There are the mickey-takers. And there are people who praise him – nothing wrong in that, you might feel, except that footballers tend sometimes to think such admirers are after something in return.

Young people in Sammy's position have to be careful. He worries, for instance, about what his future would hold if injury cut short his career. Some kind of business, or investment, might appear to be the answer, but as he says, 'As a footballer you meet a lot of people and it's difficult sorting out the genuine ones when everyone seems to want to make you a millionaire.' He doesn't have an agent, or an adviser as they are often called. 'If I am asked to make a presentation or something, and I can, I'll go – and that's it. It's not that I don't want an agent, but to be honest I'm still concentrating on getting my football sorted out. I feel that, if I get that right, other things will come along.' Someone told him recently that Kevin Keegan didn't have an agent until he was 27 and he found it reassuring – 'You can't have a better yardstick than Kevin.'

At times Sammy can seem over-critical of his own performance, questioning, criticizing and analysing after every match, but that is only because his ambitions are pitched high. He doesn't want to be branded as a hard-working rather than a skilful player, rightly believing that industry is only part of his game. He wants to be recognized as an England player and says: 'I have to have pride in what I do. It won't last for ever and I want to be the best. *I know I never will be* but I must want to be. It's a case of so far, so good, but I have a long way to go. And it's why the only advisers I am taking notice of at the moment are my football advisers – the Liverpool coaching staff and my Mum and Dad.' And you can't have your feet more firmly on the ground than that.

CHAPTER FOUR

The problems of coping with First Division stardom have not yet affected Micky Phelan, though if they ever do this likeable twenty-one-year-old Burnley defender can be expected to confront them with the same brand of common sense that has brought his career along very satisfactorily so far. Unlike Steve Coppell or Sammy Lee, he has come through every one of the orthodox stages of a young footballer's development, starting as an associate schoolboy with Burnley, whose scouts began to take an interest in Micky when he was only 12 years old. He is, of course, still learning the game, and even now it's sometimes a case of learning the hard way.

For instance, he had to suffer the disappointment of missing the last two months of Burnley's campaign for promotion to the Second Division in 1982 after fracturing a cheekbone in a match against Wimbledon. It wasn't a dirty match, he says, which implies that in the fiercely competitive Third Division the elbow an opponent smashed into his face after the ball had gone was far from unusual. The lesson he took from that incident was simple: 'I told myself I would never get hurt in the same way again, I'd make sure I got in first in future. I wouldn't deliberately hurt anyone I was playing against, but I'd go in hard and win the ball in such a way that I came out on top. In other words, it made me tougher.' That is the sort of response the professional clubs like to hear.

It's typical of Micky, according to Gordon Clayton, assistant manager at Turf Moor, who describes him as a 'Rolls-Royce' among young footballers. He considers Micky is a near certainty to do well in the game, because his ability is coupled with determination and a sense of responsibility. Tom Saunders of Liverpool described earlier the critical stage experienced by players who come to prominence as schoolboys and have their heads turned. Well, Micky survived it. Yet the temptations to become carried away with his progress were there, because at 14, when he became officially associated with Burnley, he was heavily in demand. Most of the Lancashire clubs – Blackburn Rovers, Bolton Wanderers, Oldham Athletic – were interested, as well as Queens Park Rangers from further afield.

He chose Burnley because they were his home-town club and he had always supported them. It was a happy choice. The Turf Moor club have splendid facilities, and a tradition of producing young players. Once the Turf Moor staff had had a look at Micky, they never doubted that he would do less than go on to be an apprentice. His reminiscences of his period as an apprentice might indicate that the life, certainly at Burnley, is more appropriate to the education of a groundsman than a footballer. However, Burnley's record of success in grooming their own players speaks for itself. The apprentices, who are paid about £30 a week plus an allowance for board and lodgings, work as a team and their routine involves such tasks as cleaning boots, tidying the stands and terraces, and rolling the pitch. They also have to replace divots after matches, which can mean working late into the night if there's frost about and the job cannot wait until morning.

The training sessions are supervised by the youth coach and in Micky's time this was Frank Casper, who is now Burnley's manager. Casper was succeeded by Ray Pointer, and Ray by Arthur Bellamy, all former Burnley players, following the club's tradition of keeping it in the family as much as possible. As Micky says, 'It's a homely club.' At the apprentice stage, players begin to have their first occasional training sessions with the seniors and Micky found the likes of Martin Dobson, Jim Thomson, and Billy Rodaway quick to offer a warm welcome and ready advice on how to make the most of his career. 'They are all good, experienced professionals,' says Micky, 'and I always try to follow their example now that I am in the first team. When a young lad comes to the club from school I talk to him and ask him about himself. I know it did me good when I was his age. So I am passing it on – keeping a club tradition going really.'

This is not to say that the professionals are slow to put the youngsters in their place from time to time, maybe with a sharp reminder that there are boots waiting to be cleaned. Nor are they above trying to catch them out with a practical joke. As an example, Micky recalls the embarrassment of poor Billy O'Rourke, the young newly promoted goalkeeper who conceded seven goals on his debut against Queens Park Rangers at Loftus Road in 1979. The following week Burnley were back in London to play Orient and as the players relaxed in their hotel the night before the match one of them rang O'Rourke from another room. Disguising his voice, while others suppressed their giggles in the background, he said he was a reporter who had been very interested in O'Rourke's unfortunate experience the previous week and wanted to do an interview. Could Billy be in the foyer in half an hour? The players were counting on O'Rourke, who had never been the subject of a newspaper's attention before, taking it seriously. And he did. He showered, dressed very smartly with a collar and tie, and – making sure that every hair was in place – went down to the foyer right on time. He had been waiting a quarter of an hour when the lads burst in, howling with laughter.

The apprentices have plenty of laughs too, though they have to be careful not to apply too light-hearted an attitude to the job. As Micky says, 'You have to go through a point where you become determined and realize that, if you don't look after yourself, nobody else will. You have to drive yourself if you want to be successful. You have to decide not to stay out after 11 o'clock at night, not to have the couple of drinks or whatever your mates may be fancying. Any young lad of 18 likes to go out. I do. But one drink leads to another and it does catch up on you. It limits you.'

Micky has obviously learned to control his social life, but not everybody does and he was concerned at one point that his brother, Marcus, might become one of the drop-outs. 'He was an apprentice at Burnley, and was finding it difficult to adjust. He liked to go out enjoying himself without thinking that in two years' time it might not be the same. It was hard to get through to him. At the end of the day he might not get taken on, I told him, and he'd wonder what'd hit him. I've seen it happen to so many lads who have got released, not through footballing ability, but through what they have done outside the game – being in late mainly. The club always finds out. People ring in and say "I've seen so-and-so with a pint in his hand." It happens a lot. There are some very nice people around!' Fortunately Marcus survived, and in the spring of 1983 signed a one-year contract.

Like so many of the game's most admired young professionals – Sammy Lee, for example – Micky comes from a close, happy family and clearly he was hoping that Marcus would be able to prove his concern groundless. He wanted his brother to enjoy the marvellous moment that every apprentice prays for – the revelation that the club are keeping you on as a full professional. It happened to Micky in the summer of 1980, and was no surprise because he had recently broken into the reserve team and felt confident. The coaches had told him that, while the decision was up to the then manager, Brian Miller, he must have a good chance. Their faith was justified when Miller called Micky to his office one day and said: 'After giving it some thought, we have decided to take you on as a professional.' The manager stretched out his hand, wished Micky luck, and offered him terms that were then put on a contract and sent to his home.

A young player's first contract will usually mean his apprentice's wage being at least doubled, but Micky was not thinking about money at that particular time. He uses the footballer's favourite phrase, 'I was over the moon. I can't describe it any other way. Being taken on as an apprentice was one thing, but signing professional was the real break-through.'

Stepping up to the reserves from the Burnley youth team meant playing football that was less rushed, more methodical. 'There was time and space,' he says, 'and you were performing against better players in the Central League. I remember facing some of the famous old heads, such as Jimmy Greenhoff of Manchester United and Kevin Hector of Derby County, and I really enjoyed it. I looked forward to giving them a good game. They don't exactly push themselves to the limit at reserve level, players of that standard, so you always have a chance against them.'

Micky, meanwhile, continued to give everything to his own game and towards the end of his first season as a full professional he reached the first team. Playing alongside Martin Dobson in the Third and Second Divisions was every bit as enjoyable as he had expected, above all because of the crowds. 'It's a big difference,' he says. 'You play in front of 50 or 60 people with the youth team, then maybe 200 with the reserves, and now it's 10,000. It stimulates you, and it's bound to improve your game.' A young man who feeds off atmosphere so hungrily should have a bright future so long as he continues to learn. The need to do so is not lost on Micky, who realizes: 'Going through the motions every week would give me no chance at all. My game would not improve. And if you are a trier you always have a chance of being noticed. Clubs are always looking for hard workers.'

Among the things he is having to learn are the tricks of the professional trade, some more creditable than others. 'In the Third Division, for instance, I found that opponents will hit you off the ball a lot for no reason at all. It's just aggression. They'll just elbow you in the face – and that's how I got my fractured cheekbone. So you have to learn how to protect yourself.' There is also that most detested facet of the game, the so-called professional foul, which the football authorities are now rightly trying to stamp out. Micky says: 'If somebody was going past me and I thought he was maybe going to score, I'd whip him down. It happens a lot, particularly when promotion or relegation are at stake, but I don't like doing it and I'm glad the authorities have done something about it because there is nothing more frustrating for the spectators than that sort of thing. Let's face it, it's the spectators who pay for professional football to take place.'

Talking to Micky, it is easy to understand the high opinion of him held by Gordon Clayton, an experienced judge of talent who worked with Tommy Docherty at Manchester United and Derby County. Micky has every right to be pleased with his progress so far. He says that ideally he would like to remain at Turf Moor for the rest of his career, with the club he used to support from the terraces, but as a professional he has to keep a slightly open mind. 'If I improve,' he says, 'and other clubs fancy me and make an offer, and if in the meantime Burnley's progress is not being continued, I'd have to consider it. Because being relegated only twelve months after we got into the Second Division was very disappointing. My ambition is to play in the First Division. Every player's should be.'

CHAPTER FIVE

Another young man who wanted First Division football, and thought he could get it, was Tony Burke. Today, however, Tony works for the fire service and plays for Radcliffe St Mary's in the Bolton Combination. A highly talented forward, he was an apprentice with Blackburn Rovers for little over twelve months before being released on 3 September, 1981 – close to his eighteenth birthday – because in the club's view he lacked the aggression and determination necessary to become a professional footballer.

The decision was made by Alan Bradshaw, Blackburn's youth development officer, who says, 'He had a lot of ability. I have seen lads with far less technical skill than Tony make it as a player. But football is a game of passion. You must be passionate about wanting to succeed. You need an inner drive, an inner motivation to prove that you are better than the man you are playing against, even if it means getting hurt in the process. And I do not believe that anyone can put that into your character if it's not already there.'

Tony has reconciled himself to the decision that punctured his dream. He is not bitter, for as his father, Jim, says with a grin, 'He's too nice a lad to be a professional footballer.' Tony's story nevertheless provides a revealing insight into the apprentice's life as experienced by a member of the vast majority – the ones who fail. It began, of course, with the heady, innocent pleasure of youthful success. At the age of 14 Tony played for an excellent Bury boys' team that reached the final of the Manchester Evening News Trophy, an event which always attracts scouts. He was already an associate schoolboy with Blackburn, but a couple of other clubs then became interested. Tony was confident that he could make a career in the game and his school studies took second place. He passed CSEs in seven subjects, but mostly at Grade Two, and he reflects that he would probably have done better without the distraction of football.

At the time, however, football did not seem a distraction, more a prospective career, especially when Blackburn engaged him as an apprentice on leaving school. He was paid £25 a week, with an additional £20 going directly to his landlady in the town. He found the work at Ewood Park harder than he had expected, though he was glad to do it because, as he wistfully recalls, 'It was guided towards making me a star.' He started at nine o'clock, either doing the boots or – depending on which day it was – cleaning, folding, and neatly setting out the forty sets of kit. He trained from ten until twelve, sometimes returning for another session in the afternoon before resuming the familiar chores. He went back to his digs at about half five every weekday, except for the occasional Friday when the apprentices were given an afternoon off and went for a walk around the centre of Blackburn.

On Saturdays he was usually in the A team, which often meant getting into Ewood Park at half past nine and preparing the kit ready for kick-off at half ten. When the match was over he began work on getting the kit ready for the first team or the reserves, depending on which was at home. Finally, after watching the match, he cleaned up and could expect to leave the ground at about half six to begin the trek back to his parents' home in Bury where he spent Saturday nights.

'It was a very long week,' he says, recalling that, because

the bus service between Bury and Blackburn was so restricted, he had to return to his digs in Blackburn on Sunday nights ready for the following morning. 'But it became a little easier when I reached the reserve team and, anyway, I wasn't complaining. After all, it was just a step on the road to reaching the First Division – I honestly thought that was where I was going.'

He had, it seemed, every reason to be confident. His skills were undoubted, whether he played on the wing or in midfield, and during the latter period of his apprenticeship he did reach the reserve team, which is usually a good sign. Further evidence that the club were planning to offer him a contract as a full professional came when his eighteenth birthday approached. He was going on holiday with his parents and had booked the same fortnight as the apprentices had taken the previous year. In 1981, however, the Football League had moved the season back a fortnight and Mr Burke felt that, in the circumstances, he should ask Blackburn if Tony should change his holiday plans accordingly. He spoke to Alan Bradshaw, who said, 'Yes, otherwise it might cause problems.' This made Tony quite optimistic, but his father was still doubtful and went back to Bradshaw for another word. The answer was that the holiday could go ahead as planned. 'And when I came back from holiday,' says Tony, 'they told me. They sent for me and my Dad. I realized what they could be about to tell me. The thoughts that passed through my mind were about another lad who had been on trial and who burst into tears when they told him he could go home. I remembered thinking at the time "If that ever happens to me, there's no way I'm going to show it." So I just looked Bradshaw straight in the eye – or would have done, but he was looking down at the desk – and he said "I'm sorry, Tony, but we can't keep you on." I tried not to show any emotion. But I was very disappointed.'

Nor did the disappointment end there for, in an attempt to bounce back and reclaim his career, Tony went to Bury, his local Fourth Division club, and asked one of the coaches, Wilf McGuinness, for a trial. The former Manchester United manager said, 'No, we've got too many trialists already.' Tony pointed out that he had played two dozen matches in the reserve team at Blackburn Rovers, a Second Division club, and said, 'You can't have too many trialists like that.' McGuinness said, 'We have still got too many. Come back another time.' That was enough for Tony, who says, 'They couldn't even give me a trial – and I wouldn't mind but we had murdered Bury down at Gigg Lane not long before. And I had a good game!'

Now that the passage of time has done something to heal his wounded pride, Tony has accepted the reasons he was not offered a contract by Blackburn, but he still cannot help wondering from time to time if the club made a mistake, pointing out: 'The situation at the time was a little unusual. Howard Kendall had left and gone to Everton and the new manager, Bobby Saxton, wasn't there yet. Perhaps if Kendall had stayed, who knows what would have happened? The new manager hadn't even seen me play ...' And he smiles, 'I must have been bad!'

The others in Tony's group of five apprentices had mixed fortunes. Only one, in fact, was kept on for an extra year, and it may have been that the club had felt an obligation to him because he was still in plaster after breaking a leg in a match. Another was released for the familiar reason that late nights came above football in his list of priorities. 'He used to stay out all hours,' says Tony, 'often not getting back to the digs at all. He didn't get drunk, but he had a girlfriend and he used to go and see her. He wasn't too bothered about football, just enjoying himself. The club let him go, and he didn't seem to care.' Tony certainly cared, but maybe not in the assertive way that clubs look for.

A player with a comparatively mild temperament can be successful in the senior game, but as Alan Bradshaw makes clear he generally needs not only exceptional talent, like Glenn Hoddle's, but exceptional pace. Tony, Bradshaw feels, could not come to terms with the physical demands of the game, the need to tackle and compete for the ball. 'He had a lot of ability, was quiet, intelligent and a very nice lad who gave you no problems whatsoever. But the difference between him and the lad who gets kept on is simply the courage and confidence born of a passion to do well. He was unlucky, in a way, that his birthday fell in September so that he had only twelve months as an apprentice, whereas boys who are born in, say, June, get two seasons in which to make the difficult transition from schoolboy footballer to professional. With some lads it takes six months just to rid them of the worst of their bad habits – overdoing things on the ball, mainly – that they have picked up from being the outstanding player in a school team. Tony started with us in September, and because some of the other lads had got a game in the Central League side and he hadn't, not because of a lack of ability but because of circumstances, he seemed to throw in the towel, rather than grit his teeth and say, "I'll show them", as the more determined lad would do. I had quite a few chats with him about it, and he understood and agreed with me, but in my opinion you can't change a person's character.'

Tony, for his part, feels that it was not a lack of the will to be successful that let him down. 'I had ambition, there was no doubt about that. But at the end of the day it was confidence I was struggling for. It's difficult to analyse. Everyone always told me I'd got a lot of skill. I never had any problems with my technique and when we watched Glenn Hoddle on television my Dad always turned to me and said,

"What can he do that you can't?" But my Dad also told me that I lacked a bit of aggression, though, so I suppose that was probably it.' In this vital facet of the game lies the most significant difference between Tony, who dropped out, and Mike Phelan, who has made it to League level. Tony puts it candidly: 'In my opinion there's a difference between being aggressive and being prepared to do what people in the professional game want you to do sometimes. If somebody's skinning you during a match and you can't beat him fairly they want you to beat him unfairly. That's not in my make-up. They never say it to your face, but you know what they want you to do. Let him know you're there, they say, or get tight on him, or don't let him turn.'

The question this raises is obvious – given the choice again, would Tony learn and adopt the 'professional' ways of combating opponents so that he could fulfil his ambition of being a footballer rather than having a job in the fire service? 'I couldn't do it,' he says, 'I might even want to do it but I just couldn't. It's the same now that I play on Sundays. People kick me and I say I'll get them back and then I get the perfect opportunity but . . .'

His father, Jim Burke, says that for this reason he was not surprised when Tony was released. 'I watched him in a lot of the games down at Blackburn,' says Mr Burke, a former amateur player, 'and if I'd have been in the club's shoes I wouldn't have signed him either. I knew the score in advance. But it was a chance he had to take or he would have regretted it for the rest of his life. He had all the necessary skills, but he's too nice. I thought it might change him when he got into the professional ranks, but it didn't. He's still a pacifist – he wouldn't kick anybody. And there's nothing wrong with that. As a man, I'd rather have him the way he is.'

CHAPTER SIX

Though Tony and his parents have no feelings of bitterness, they do still regret one aspect of the time he spent at Blackburn – the interruption to his education. It came to Tony suddenly, when he went back to Ewood Park to clear out his belongings, that he had missed out on a year's preparation for life because of his preoccupation with football. And, looking back he feels a little annoyed that the club did not give him different advice. 'When you sign as a schoolboy they say "Join us and you'll be able to go to college" and all that. And, true enough, when I got to Blackburn a bloke came round from the college and told me all the courses that were available. I was not sure which course to take, so I asked Alan Bradshaw about it. He said, "Well, it's 25 per cent of your working week gone if you have a day off to go to college – and don't forget you're the oldest of the lads, you haven't got that much time to become a footballer." I said, "All right, I won't go to college then." But after you leave the club, things like that keep echoing back and you reflect that maybe you made a mistake. If you don't get a good education you can find it difficult to come by a job. As it was, I was lucky enough to be able to get into the fire service because I'm not thick and I was able to pass their entrance exams which happened to be mainly in the subjects I was good at in school – physics, maths, and so on.' Tony's father, stressing that he could understand the club's point of view, agrees, 'It was a bad decision not to go to college. We realize that now.'

Looking back on the descriptions that have been given of the apprentice's busy routine, it is obvious that the club's understanding and cooperation are vital if his education is not to fall by the wayside. People like Steve Coppell, whose well-ordered minds enable them to combine top-class professional football with university, are comparatively rare – at least outside Old Trafford, where goalkeeper Gary Bailey has gained a part-time degree course at the local polytechnic. Meanwhile Steve, armed with his economics degree, is working odd afternoons at the office of his accountant just to learn the rudiments of the job. He says, 'When I leave football I want to be able to sit down and have a number of options to consider. But, apart from that I love learning and I find that there's no real conflict with being a player. In fact I'm convinced that it helps my football by taking my thoughts off it. Football is an intuitive game, as far as I am concerned, and it's good to bring a fresh brain to it, even if that brain is tired from other things.' Even Steve might nevertheless have drifted away from the enlightened path he has taken but for the wise advice of Tommy Docherty at the time when he was considering leaving university to concentrate on football. 'You'd be stupid if you did,' said Docherty, when Steve told him of his plans, 'There's no problem – just come and train when you want.'

Every player feels the pressure to neglect his education, and the trouble with apprentices is that so many fall victim to it. Even if a youngster is making his way with one of the more constructive clubs, such as Burnley, it's difficult to keep up with the courses that are available. Mike Phelan failed to get a pass in the course he took, for as he says, 'The classes often involve midweek day-release and nights. They always seem to fall on Tuesdays and Wednesdays, and it's hard luck if you have a midweek game. You can't go – the club just won't let you go. Therefore you get further and further behind, and you find you can't pick up what has been missed in terms of taking notes and so on – and so you just drop out.' Mike is in the fortunate position that, barring serious injury, he has every likelihood of remaining fully employed in the game for many years. Time is on his side. But he admits, 'If I fell out of the game right now I'd be struggling. I've got a couple of O-levels, and that's all. I don't know what I'd do. I'd be stuck. Most players would.'

Among the people working hardest to help such players safeguard their futures is Bob Kerry, football's education officer. Bob runs a scheme rejoicing in the none-too-snappy title of the Footballers' Further Education and Vocational Training Society. He is based at the offices of the Professional Footballers' Association – the players' union – in Hanging Ditch, Manchester, though the scheme is managed and paid for jointly by the P.F.A. and the Football League. It began in 1979. Bob's job is to provide an advisory service helping footballers of all ages to prepare for the day when they finish playing.

Bob understands only too well the feelings of prospective apprentices who might be doing well at school but cannot resist the temptation to gamble everything on football. 'It is very rare,' he says, 'that the boy will say to a club "Thank you for the offer of an apprenticeship, but I prefer to stay on at school and go to sixth-form college." The boy who does that is the boy who has got his head screwed on. But I will say this – if, when I was 16, my local club Bolton Wanderers had come in for me, no power on earth would have stopped me from signing. And I wouldn't have wanted any wages or anything like that. So I recognize how the lads feel.'

The facts of life, however, are that more than 50 per cent

of apprentices are not offered contracts by clubs – and that, of those who are lucky enough to be offered contracts, a further 50 per cent find themselves out of the professional game by the time they reach the age of 22. Those young players who disregard the need for some kind of education are, therefore, doing themselves no favours at all. Part of Bob's role is to visit the clubs and talk to their players, assessing their various individual needs. They do not always take his advice, believing as Tony Burke did that taking a course might sidetrack their development as footballers. But an increasing number are taking advantage of the grants available under Bob's scheme, which paid out a total of £54,000 in course fees alone during 1981/2 – more than treble the corresponding figure for two years earlier.

The courses are usually at colleges, polytechnics, or special trade schools and cover an almost infinite variety of subjects. A player might learn a trade or qualify in business studies with the intention of starting a small firm. Or even, if he has plans to stay in the game as one in forty footballers do, follow the example of Terry Venables, Alan Durban, Roy McFarland and many others in taking the residential course in football management run in conjunction with the St Helens School of Management Studies. The courses are being taken up not only by apprentices, then, but also by full-time, established professionals eager to plan a new career for the time when they have to retire.

Bob's advice has to be carefully considered, as in the case of Geoff Nulty, the former Burnley, Newcastle United and Everton defender, who became assistant manager of Preston North End. Bob describes Geoff as 'one of our typical success stories'. He had left school at 18 with two A-levels, quickly obtained another, and began a part-time degree course at Burnley Technical College. It was, says Bob, 'wrong, totally wrong for him ... he was bored to tears'. It didn't help that

Young Burnley star, Micky Phelan (*Eamonn McCabe*)

FOUR MOMENTS IN THE CAREER

11-year-old Dennis Tueart (*left, standing*) takes a football proficiency test, 1961

A member of Sunderland's First Division team, 1969–70. Tueart, aged 19, is second from left, front row

OF AN ENGLAND INTERNATIONAL:

Wedding day (*above*).
The best man was Brian
Chambers (*top centre*),
a former schoolboy
star with more natural
talent than Tueart,
but less determination
(*John Learwood*)

Now a star with
Manchester City (*right*)
(*Eamonn McCabe*)

Steve Coppell (*opposite, top, holding ball*), captain of his school team, 1964–5

And in an England jersey (*opposite, bottom*), pursued by Chris McGrath of Northern Ireland. McGrath's experience shows the perils of professional football: despite spells with First Division clubs Spurs and Manchester United, he has now faded from the scene (*Eamonn McCabe*)

Bobby Robson (*above*), former manager of Ipswich, now manager of the England team (*Eamonn McCabe*)

Tony Cottee (*left*), aged 11, after winning the Essex Cup with his team, Romford Royals
And six years later (*below*), in the England Youth strip. The small trophy is for ending up as leading scorer in a Yugoslav International Youth tournament (September 1982), which England won; the large trophy for West Ham's Young Player of the Year Award, 1981–2
Cottee battles with Tottenham's Gary O'Reilly (*opposite, right*) in a First Division game (*Steve Bacon*)
Cottee's team-mate, Alan Dickens (*below*), established himself in the West Ham first team early in 1983 – he is shown here in action against Sunderland (*Steve Bacon*)

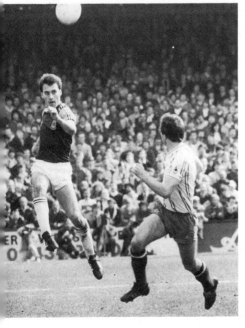

England international Sammy Lee, in his Liverpool club strip (*Eamonn McCabe*)

Geoff had missed lectures because of football commitments, causing large gaps to appear in his notes. Eventually he abandoned the course. 'I then talked to Geoff,' says Bob, 'and put him in touch with someone who advised the Open University. It wasn't exactly easy for him, with his wife giving birth to three children during the years he was studying, and there were two changes of club for him as well, but he worked when he could – often into the small hours of the morning – and in 1981 he graduated.'

Another splendid achievement was that of Gordon Taylor, now the P.F.A. Secretary, who battled on for seven years during his playing career with Bolton Wanderers, eventually gaining an external degree in economics from London University. Gordon attended a college in Manchester whenever possible, but promotion to the first team made it difficult at times and he had to get by largely on instruction by correspondence. Once he broke an arm, and had to rely on other students' note-taking, and at one stage a clash between exams and a club tour nearly resulted in a transfer. It was something of an obstacle course for Gordon, but he got his prize in the end – and became a dynamic and highly respected leader of the players' trade union. In the last ten years the number of players taking courses has increased and Bob Kerry says the most pleasing development has been among the older players, more and more of whom are committing themselves to good quality courses in the way Geoff Nulty did.

The position of apprentices is rather different. They have an established right to continue their education if they wish, but with some clubs making it more difficult than others the growth in the number of apprentices who persevere with their studies on a day-release basis is not as fast as Bob would like to see. Around half the League clubs have appointed education officers, who might be the chief scout, or the youth team coach, or perhaps someone from outside such as a local headmaster. In some cases it can be a well-known figure such as Watford's Bertie Mee, the manager of the double-winning Arsenal team of 1971. Bertie is one of an increasing number of individuals in football who are beginning to recognize their responsibilities towards young players. Bob pays tribute to him and to Tom Saunders, who 'would never let a Liverpool lad miss out on education if he wanted it'. Among the other clubs who have good reputations in this respect he names Tottenham Hotspur, Watford, Arsenal, Leicester City, Leeds United, Luton Town, Burnley, Bristol Rovers, Charlton Athletic, and Port Vale. 'It's still very patchy,' he says, 'but it's getting better.'

Education for young footballers should not, however, be seen simply as a matter of obtaining a diploma or learning a trade that will help when they eventually leave the game. There are some interesting courses around. One of the best examples was to be found at Brathay Hall on the north shore of Windermere in the Lake District. There the apprentices of several clubs including Everton, Ipswich Town, Derby County, Newcastle United and Port Vale were sent to learn how to improve their performance – in the same way as trainee technicians and managers have been sent from a variety of other industries. They spend most of the time outside, mountaineering, orienteering, and canoeing – though the image of an Outward Bound school was a misleading one according to Chris Hillman, who directed the course. 'It was a psychological exercise as much as anything else,' he explains. 'The aim was to teach things like initiative and communication. It was designed to relate directly to developing football technique that is not primarily concerned with the ball – like teamwork, motivation, and problem-solving. The boys were expected to work things out for themselves.'

As a former associate schoolboy with West Bromwich Albion, Chris knows all about the failure rate in football, and he firmly believes that such courses can help a young player to avoid being one of the drop-outs. Bob Kerry agrees and has given every assistance by providing grants for clubs who send groups of apprentices on youth training schemes. 'I think it's a good thing,' he says, 'but more importantly so do managers like John McGrath at Port Vale. Nobody could accuse big John, who is one of the game's real characters, of being a wishy-washy educationalist but he says Brathay did his lads the world of good.' John McGrath gives as examples a young goalkeeper, previously too shy to 'boss' his penalty area, who began to order his defenders about like a sergeant-major after attending Brathay, and another boy who was released by the club but was then able to obtain a job in engineering with the help of his course report. This impresses Bob Kerry, who draws a parallel between the Brathay course and management studies: 'It's nearly all common sense, but like the sort of thing that is taught in management studies it's the sort of common sense people are otherwise inclined to overlook. It's learning how to cope with problems, to take responsibility. To give an example, they had a raft-building exercise at Brathay, and it was a cracker. They gave the lads a couple of oil drums and some pieces of wood and said "Get over to that island." It was suggested in advance that they appoint a leader. There's a simple little lesson that, even if your leader isn't the best in the world, the fact that you have a leader who says "Do this, do that" makes you a more efficient unit than if you were a set of brilliant individuals. It's common sense, yes, but then so is football to a considerable extent.'

CHAPTER SEVEN

Even Brathay's most ardent admirers would not pretend that such courses could make a footballer. All they can do is hope to improve one or, if that is not enough, to provide him with a career in the game, to make him better prepared for life in general. Young footballers, because of the temptations to inhabit what Tom Saunders called a 'fool's paradise', neglecting education and other points of contact with the mainstream of life, often lead a rather artificial existence.

Someone who is determined to do something about this is Tricia Hesketh, who runs a course specially designed for footballers. It teaches them everything from cookery to how to handle a press interview, write a letter, or even start their own business. Tricia's is one of only a handful of such enterprises throughout the country – there have been others in London and Cardiff – but Bob Kerry is enthusiastic about them and says they are slowly catching on. The courses are paid for by the Government through the Manpower Services Commission, which gives grants to clubs. The idea came from Tricia, who is a lecturer in English, History, and other subjects at Bury College of Further Education – and, in her spare time, a keen football supporter. She realized that many players must be dropping out of football at a young age, or having to finish their careers early because of injury, or even finding themselves jobless on retiring from the game in their thirties. She felt that since football is a large feature of life in the north-west, her college should be catering for it in some way. She wrote to the Professional Footballers' Association, and when Bob and Gordon Taylor immediately became interested she outlined her plans for the course, which had three parts:

1. Science – anatomy, sport injuries, nutrition, and so on.
2. Practical experiments – such things as woodwork, car maintenance, and cookery, as well as coaching and refereeing.
3. Life and social skills – concerned with 'survival', budgeting, job interviews, and the important matter of dealing with the public, which a footballer must learn to do if he is to give a good impression of himself and his club.

Tricia's view is that footballers may have more to learn than they realize – including plain, simple, good manners. 'Basically,' she says, 'we are trying to give them independence, because footballers are used to having everything done for them – travel arrangements and so on – and they tend to be lost when thrown into the outside world. We are trying to help them to adjust, because I've found footballers are really very different from the other young people I deal with at the college. In fact, I would go so far as to say that ninety per cent of those I have met – of all ages, and at all levels – are ill-mannered, inconsiderate and thoughtless in their behaviour towards other people. I teach young people from other occupations, such as engineers, and they are not the same. For instance, I have yet to come across a young engineer who will come into a class late without excusing himself or apologizing. Most footballers would. But they soon alter their ways after I have been teaching them for six weeks or so.'

There are exceptions. Tricia singles out Micky Phelan as a good pupil – 'he didn't need any lessons in good manners from me or anyone else' – and says she has been particularly pleased with Burnley's response to the course. In 1981/2 about half of her forty pupils came from Turf Moor, including the talented Trevor Steven and four other members of the first-team squad. The rest came from the Manchester clubs, Oldham Athletic, Bury, and Bolton Wanderers. She has been a little disappointed with the response of some of the bigger clubs. 'Their boys are spoiled, cushioned from reality, most of all – they are the ones who most need it. Joe Brown, the youth development officer at Manchester United, and Tony Book at City have tried to make the boys realize they should be attending – Tony even fines them for missing classes – but the attitude of most of the boys is that it's a waste of time. And, sadly, many of the senior professionals support them. Martin Buchan and Lou Macari are two who have been helpful, but they are in a minority. Other players, and coaches, and managers, have told me the boys should be concentrating on their football, or cleaning the ground and doing the other jobs traditionally expected of apprentices.'

Nevertheless the numbers attending continue to grow from the eleven who came to the first course in 1979. Only four finished that time, but last year Manchester United were the only club whose apprentices dropped out of the scheme. Tricia says clubs have an obligation towards boys who have perhaps been taken away from home and put into an unfamiliar environment. They may not be particularly polite, nor able to express themselves, but the other side of the coin is the pressure they are under. They have just left school and are being asked to do a lot of unfamiliar things, get used to a group of unfamiliar people, and prove they can be footballers. And there are restrictions, particularly for boys brought up in a different area from the club. As Tricia says: 'Girlfriends don't always understand that you can't go out on a Friday night.' The clubs tend to find apprentices good landladies who can cook good food – and then assume that there will be no problems with homesickness. Tricia says, 'I have had to ring clubs and say, "Look, I think your player is suffering from homesickness. Can you give him a few days back with his family?" And they say, "Oh, that's what's wrong with him? Fair enough, then." But they do need telling.' Again she makes an exception of Burnley, who automatically send all their apprentices home for a few days every month. They also try to create a family atmosphere, with the players' parents and landladies being encouraged to attend matches. But even in the best-run clubs, says Tricia, a lot of boys will be uneasy about going to a member of the coaching staff with a problem, for fear that a black mark will be put against his career.

Though Tricia feels that the clubs could do more in the way of offering advice, she recognizes that their attitude is governed by what they want from the boys. They want a player, and if he's not going to make it he's out. Indeed some of the professionals believe that Tricia, in alerting boys to the future, is doing them a disservice by disillusioning them about football. The more starry-eyed the boys are, the harder they will work at becoming players, or so the theory goes. Tricia disagrees, saying, 'The last thing I want to do is remove their dreams. But they must be aware that their careers are going to end at some time, even if it's not until they are 35.'

One characteristic Tricia has noticed about apprentices in particular is how little they know about other people's lives outside football. So she tries to get her pupils to mix with students from other walks of life as much as possible. She is trying to show them that they have a relationship with – and responsibilities to – the community. Many people feel that, with football clubs becoming less able to survive financially and crowds dropping, there is a need for players to work harder off the field. Some clubs, including Burnley, have encouraged players to do coaching sessions with schoolboys, which not only helps the boys but gives them an interest in the club. The players of the future may indeed have to become ambassadors as well as learning the other techniques of professionalism. And they certainly have the time according to Tricia, who says, 'Footballers are under-employed, they know it, and in my experience they want to do more. Vince Overson, who was in my class at Burnley, calculated that first-team professionals work about 15 hours a week on average – and the whole class was horrified.'

Although the point of the classes is for the footballers to learn from Tricia, she has learned plenty from them, especially the differences in their characters. Her experience supports the professional view that toughness, psychologically as well as on the pitch, is almost always required for success. 'The lads who are fairly pleasant and easy-going are not always successful. In football you often need to fight hard, for instance to get your place back if you are dropped. And you need to be able to withstand the amount of adverse, often unkind, often insensitive criticism you will have thrown at you, and rise above it.' And yet she is teaching people to be polite citizens at the same time? 'I don't see why the two should be incompatible. You can stand up for your own interests and work hard and be determined not to let petty things get you depressed and still get on quite well with other people. You have to know your own worth. It might make you seem arrogant at times – but it gets you places.'

Tricia's aim is to help her pupils find a balance. She remembers Clayton Blackmore who came from Manchester United and was 'an absolute so-and-so as a pupil because he was going to be a good player and he knew it'. She wants to give young footballers a wider sense of their place in the community, feeling that in this small way she can aid the health of the game 'My colleagues teased me about it,' she says. 'Every time they see a monosyllabic footballer being interviewed on television they say, "Look, you're not doing much good yet, are you?" And I say, "Just wait until my generation start appearing on television, like Trevor Steven and the others – you'll see."'

CHAPTER EIGHT

The number of players with Football League clubs who have bypassed – or perhaps been ignored by – the conventional scouting network is high and shows no sign of declining. They are sometimes called the late developers. Among them are Cyrille Regis, aged 18 when West Bromwich Albion's Ronnie Allen plucked him from near obscurity, and Alan Devonshire who was 20 and driving fork-lift trucks for a living before Southall's loss became West Ham United's gain. In the recent past there were such stars as Steve Heighway, who was 23 when he emerged with startling brilliance at Liverpool after playing for several years with the top amateur club Skelmersdale United while studying for a university degree at Warwick. As a teenager Steve did catch the eye of one or two professional clubs. Indeed he trained two nights a week with Manchester City at one stage. But he was not offered professional forms at Maine Road and until Bill Shankly came on the scene he fully intended to use his degree to become a teacher.

Countless others have come into the professional game late, casting doubt perhaps on the advisability of clubs concentrating their scouting effort on boys of tender years. Dennis Tueart says it amazes him. He joined his first club, Sunderland, as a teenager, having gone through most of the orthodox stages, but during his long career he has seen so many boys drop out because their mental and physical development between the ages of 14 and 18 failed to keep pace with their skills. It would be impossible to calculate the percentage who make it as professionals after being spotted at 14, but few would deny that the answer would be very low.

Dennis thinks the question of mental development is especially important. 'You need character,' he says – and the younger players at Manchester City will appreciate that he says it with some feeling! Dennis has not been slow to offer advice to the likes of Ray Ranson, the right-back at Maine Road, who has captained the England Under 21 team but, like almost every footballer, has experienced the ups and downs. Dennis says, 'I am always on to Ray about this business of character-building. He had a few traumatic times in the 1981/2 season and every time he bounced back, I would just say to him, "It's another brick in the wall." That's how I see the life of a professional footballer. You are building a wall that is going to be the basis of your career. And you build most of it in your youth.'

He gives the apprentice's life as a prime example of the need to show 'character' at an early age. Not everyone finds it as easy to cope as, for instance, Micky Phelan did at Burnley with his natural advantages, and his friends and family close at hand. Apprentices are often taken away from their schoolfriends at 16 or 17 and thrown into a wider world where, says Dennis, people might not care whether they get hurt or not. They have to achieve something on their own, and the ones who are successful are those who adjust mentally to the professional world. 'All of a sudden you are not being mollycoddled; people are not playing up to you; people are no longer sympathizing with you; you are no longer the young star of the school team. You look for sympathy and don't get it. You have to start picking yourself up. And this is where determination, the vital factor, comes in. It can then become the foundation of your career.'

To illustrate his point Dennis tells the story of two young hopefuls from Newcastle who started out together on the road to the top, back in the Sixties. One was Brian Chambers, whose League career ended with a spell at Halifax Town on loan from A.F.C. Bournemouth at the end of the 1981/2 season. And the other was Dennis himself. They were close friends from the age of 12 and both went on to play for Newcastle schoolboys.

'Brian was the star,' Dennis recalls. 'All the clubs in the country were after him. But he wanted to stay on at school and take a few more exams, so he chose to sign associate schoolboy forms for Sunderland, who were close by. At 14 I had not grown at all, so my chances were limited, but Sunderland decided to sign me as well, on amateur forms. Brian and I would go through to Sunderland from Newcastle together on Tuesday and Thursday evenings and we would play for the junior team on Saturday. Now Brian had loads of natural ability, and what's more he'd developed physically, so he was the top boy in the area – and I was just a little fighter! But we stayed together and were both offered professional forms at seventeen and a half. Around that time we had a conversation I will always remember. It took place one night at a bus stop. We'd just got off the bus at Newcastle after travelling back from Roker and we were talking about attitude – to the extent that we could discuss such matters at that time. I don't know why, but I asked Brian "If you and I were fighting for a place in the side and there was only one place and it was you or me – would you kick me?" And he said "Well, I'm not sure ..." because he was a nice lad. "No," he said eventually, "I don't think I would." And I said "I'd kick you." And I wasn't saying it in a nasty way at all. Looking back, I think that probably illustrated my attitude to the game. I wanted to be successful more than anything else. Friends are friends, but competitors are competitors. And when you are a professional you are competing for a living – it isn't a game any more.'

Brian Chambers, a skilful midfield player, did not suffer the fate of many schoolboy internationals and went on to enjoy a respectable career in the game. He made 53 league appearances for Sunderland and was in their squad for the famous F.A. Cup Final of 1973 when Ian Porterfield's goal beat Leeds United, causing one of Wembley's biggest upsets. But he didn't make the team that day and the following month was transferred to Arsenal. After a short spell at Highbury, he moved to Luton Town, then Millwall, then Bournemouth, who loaned him to Halifax. Then he played for Poole Town as a part-timer.

Meanwhile Dennis, who frankly admits he was 'not in Brian's class for ability' at the age of 17, went on to gain six England caps and play in Europe and America. Football has taken him to more than fifty countries. He left the First Division, in fact, only to star for the New York Cosmos and, in the process, make enough money to ensure that his family would always be comfortable. Indeed it is difficult, looking around Dennis's beautiful home in the leafy southern suburbs of Manchester, to imagine that his young son Mark will ever have to cut out linoleum soles for his father's cast-off shoes – just to have a game of football.

If, as Mark grows up, he has any thoughts about trying to follow in father's footsteps, Dennis will give him the same advice he would give any youngster: 'It's hard. While football is an easy game to play, it's a difficult game to play well. And if you get past all the pitfalls facing the young hopeful and reach the professional ranks, every year you will be climbing hurdles while other people try to knock you down. You've got to keep pushing yourself. I did, and I like to think that's why my career has gone on well into my thirties. Some people can get away without this level of commitment, but you can count them on the fingers of one hand. There's Trevor Francis, whose attitude is nowhere near as positive as mine, and Glenn Hoddle – in a decade you might get a handful. And while kids should try, by all means, to copy the marvellous things these players can do with the ball, they must not believe they can get anywhere near the same standard without putting in tremendous effort. When I was at school I had my idols – flair players like Jim Baxter and Denis Law – but later I came to admire Alan Ball just as much because it's a game of hard work as well as skill.

'Then again, it was an education for me, when I went to New York, to see great players like Franz Beckenbauer and Carlos Alberto. They were 33 and 35 respectively, each had captained a World Cup winning team – in short they had achieved everything in the game – and yet in training and playing their attitude was still first class. They wanted to win. And that really came home to me. I used to say to myself, "This is why these guys were the best in the world for a decade." And I'm sure their attitude came from disciplining themselves from an early age. It goes back to what I was saying before about Ray Ranson. It's a matter of putting those bricks in the wall you build, which helps you fight through pain and adversity to eventual success.

'Once attitude and application are instilled in your character, once the wall is finally built, it becomes natural and you will be able to enjoy a footballer's standard of living – in many cases, a very good life.'

CHAPTER NINE

Whenever people talk about the world's great players, the name of Johan Cruyff invariably crops up. But when the discussions are among the managers and coaches of our professional clubs, their feelings about Cruyff and the other brilliant Dutchmen of the 1970s are often tinged with wistfulness. They know that, when Ajax took him on, the grateful Amsterdam club were enjoying a privilege that is denied their English counterparts. Cruyff was just 10 years old when he started playing for Ajax, who have no fewer than six junior teams – catering for youngsters between the ages of seven and fifteen – as well as their youth and full-time professional sides. The club's sense of priorities is heavily biased towards youth development, with four of their six full-time coaches concentrating on the youngsters. And the youth programme is being closely supervised by no less an authority than Cruyff himself. It is expensive, but Ajax feel that the money is well spent.

No doubt plenty of British clubs would feel the same were they given the opportunity. But here the footballing authorities state that they must not even approach a boy until he is 14, when under League directives he must be offered associate forms even to be allowed a trial. Among those who feel frustrated by this state of affairs are John Cartwright, the former England youth coach, and the Tottenham Hotspur coach Peter Shreeves, whose time with the Spurs youth team saw the emergence of Glenn Hoddle and other top players. They feel that efforts to improve the level of technique in England – which pretty well everyone in the professional game approves – will be severely handicapped until clubs are able to make contact with players of a much younger age.

Peter believes that the decline of street football has made the reform an urgent necessity, and illustrates his point with a worrying tale. He was in charge of the Spurs youth team from 1974. That year, the club took on its full quota of fifteen apprentices. And some of those they released were not, he recalls, far from the required standard. Yet in 1982 Tottenham took on just one apprentice professional. Having scoured England, Scotland, Wales and Ireland, they considered only one boy good enough – and the irony was that he came from Enfield, just a couple of miles away from their ground. 'The raw talent is just not there any more,' says Peter.

The same sense of urgency is expressed by England team manager Bobby Robson, who feels that school teachers are not always capable of giving the most expert coaching to prospective footballers. 'Most of them do a good job educationally,' he says, 'but they are simply not equipped to teach football to the highest standard. Kids are coming out of school with awful habits, and awful technique, and I honestly think that the only solution is for professional clubs to get access to the boys long before they reach 14 years of age. Why should football be different from any other skill? After all, if a child is a very good piano player it would be thought right and proper for him to go to a professional music teacher. That makes sense. If we were given a chance to teach boys, clubs like Ipswich could take a dozen of the best 10-year-olds in their towns and by the time they came out of school at 16, I could guarantee they would be far more accomplished than what's coming out of schools today.

I really do think it's a scandal that we are not allowed to do it. The time has come to break down the opposition from those senior chaps at the English Schools' Football Association who say we are going to turn the boys' minds off education. The whole point is that fooball is part of a kid's education. I'll say this – if he learns football skills, they could get him a job! There is also a feeling that some clubs would not be responsible about it. I've heard people say they wouldn't let their kid go to such-and-such a club in case he ended up a villain. Well, that's nonsense in my opinion and all I ask is that we get a chance to prove that we can do the thing properly – if it can happen in Holland I don't see why it cannot happen here. It's a crying shame . . .'

It is, indeed, difficult to imagine how people like Bobby and Peter Shreeves could be anything but a good influence on schoolboy footballers. In fact, the more you speak to some of today's managers and coaches the more you realize that they genuinely have the game's best interests at heart. They feel a need to teach the dying skills. Like Peter, many of them are natural enthusiastic teachers. 'Mind you,' he says, 'I come from a long line of them – Tottenham is a teaching club.' When he was involved with the youths out at Cheshunt they used to spend long hours working in the ball court during the afternoons. There were a lot of what the coaches call 'unopposed practices' – a ball for each player, and a brick wall. It was simple, but effective, and Peter counts himself among the school of coaches who would like to see stretches of brick wall put up throughout the playing fields and training grounds of Britain. There is, he says, nothing better than a boy kicking a ball against a wall for learning his angles, improving his first touch, and generally acquiring the ability to play football of the kind so attractively presented at White Hart Lane by Mike Hazard, Steve Perryman, and others in recent years.

Including Garth Crooks. Well, Garth was actually brought to Tottenham at great cost from Stoke City but it's worth remembering that he came to the notice of the Potteries club as a youngster when Tony Waddington, then Stoke's manager, found him practising outside the club offices – hitting a ball against the brickwork of the Victoria Ground!

Glenn Hoddle, of course, is an exceptional case, because he possesses special qualities of touch and control that have always put him in a different class from the others. He was a 'nightmare' for the youth coach because, as Peter explains, 'You would sometimes spend hours devising a programme for a particular day and then Glenn would arrive and in twenty minutes he'd have gone through it all and would be saying "What's next?" while the more normal types would still be working on the first thing you set them. My concern at the time was skill development, because first and foremost we are always aiming to get the boys comfortable on the ball, but looking back what I might have done with Glenn is taken him out and run him ten miles over the country. There you are – hindsight's a wonderful thing!'

Some of Peter's boys were inevitably better than others. Those who were able to adapt to Tottenham's standards graduated with good touch and skill. Others left the club, but although they didn't make it, at least they had the satisfaction of knowing they had enjoyed a good footballing education. One of those who benefited most markedly from it was Paul Miller, now a member of the first team. He has worked hard for his success. Peter remembers Paul coming to Tottenham as a 15-year-old: 'He was just a big, strong, raw-boned youngster, but he's grafted and grafted and carved out a very good career for himself. His skill was always suspect, and even now we work on it, but he's got an East End grit and determination that has seen him through.'

Paul was obviously a good learner, just as Alan Brazil

proved to be in his different way when he went to Ipswich. As Bobby Robson says, 'He listened to the ways we felt he could improve his game. We may all think, as managers and coaches, that we are good teachers but they have to be good pupils. All the players we produced at Ipswich – George Burley, John Wark, Eric Gates, Russell Osman, Terry Butcher, and the rest – have listened intently and taken it all in.'

The lessons, as we have been told, become harder as the player progresses to first-team level and even Tottenham, with their admirable principles, have to prepare their young hopefuls for the physical demands of League football. Peter says, 'We are known as one of the footballing sides. But what happens to the skilful young players when they get into the hurly-burly of the First Division and say "Nobody told me about this – the short-arm chop. How do I deal with that?" So at some stage you have to teach them to look after themselves as well. It's not easy to produce your skills under pressure when you get people closing you down and getting a foot in and hustling and bustling – but it has to be learned.'

This kind of talk tends to give ammunition to those in the English Schools' F.A. and elsewhere who want to keep young players away from the professional clubs. But they may be missing the real point. No one is remotely suggesting that players under the age of 14 need preparation for the unarmed combat of the League. The critics do nevertheless need convincing that Peter, Bobby, and their counterparts throughout the country are interested only in the admirable aim of improving technique. Youngsters like Steve Coppell, who from an early age were happy to practise alone for hours, will always come through, but Peter asks: 'How many? We have all seen the disappearance of street games in many areas, and although kids still have the option of working individually with the ball it can get boring for them after a while. If only we could get to them in greater numbers, the situation would be bound to improve. We don't want to ram tactics down their throats or anything like that, just to organize them into little three- or four-a-side games so that they are getting as many touches of the ball as possible. I've seen some farcical games where there are twenty-two playing and some hardly ever getting a touch. That can't be doing any good.'

If Bobby Robson succeeds in his bridge-building efforts it will open up all sorts of possibilities. For example, clubs unable to spend scarce resources on extra coaching staff to look after their new youngsters could instead give their players the opportunity of teaching the game that gave them a living. Many players already enjoy coaching, and increasingly they are being sent into the schools for a couple of afternoons a week. The clubs see these schemes as good public relations, but in terms of producing professional footballers of the future they are simply not specialized or concentrated enough to make a great deal of difference. The job needs to be done at the clubs, says Bobby, who recalls that during his days as a player with West Bromwich Albion he used to supplement his income by coaching at a local school. He recalls: 'I needed the money. I was paid £20 a week at the time, and I had a wife and kids, so I used to go to the school two afternoons a week. They gave me £2 a time – two guineas it was, actually. I enjoyed it and through teaching the kids I learned to become a coach. It stood me in good stead and I'm sure many of today's players would find the same. But just think of what they could do if it was all opened up the way we want it. It's so frustrating.'

The wise old head of Liverpool's youth programme Tom Saunders nods in sympathy with the modern coaches' concerns. What he terms 'these artificial barriers' between schools and clubs frustrate Tom more than most, in fact, because he has been on both sides of the fence. He says: 'I believe that in this country we have all the know-how anybody could wish to have. So why aren't we producing better players than we are? Largely because of these barriers that exist between schools, the professional clubs, the Sunday League clubs, and all the rest of it – if only they were torn down, then we'd set off again all the stronger. I'm sure of it.'

He doubts, however, that the professional clubs are properly equipped to deal with the highly skilled job of getting the best out of very young boys. Clubs are looking to their own interest, which is right and understandable, but Tom's concern goes wider. A former teacher, he has a dream of going back into the schools, taking all his experience, and setting about the job he believes football must tackle. He says, 'We have to sell football to the kids – something that never needed to happen in my day, when they'd walk miles for a game – and that means altering the way we teach it.' With a smile, Tom remembers the time when he got his first coaching badge. 'Oh, it gave me the magic. And the kids gathered round to get the magic from me and at the end of it a little fellow knocked me under the elbow and said, "Excuse me, Sir – when are we going to play the proper game?" I've never forgotten that. Now I'd want to go back and grade any youngsters in order of ability so that they could all enjoy the proper game. In other words the misshapen ones, the awkward ones, let them play together – let them have their small-sided game, possibly with bigger goals so that they could experience the thrill of scoring. Because what happens is that children are ruthless at school. They pick their own teams often and the lad who's not very good feels smaller and smaller because he never gets picked until the end. So grade them, and let them play enjoyable football. And don't let's have the teachers stopping and starting and saying "We're playing 4-2-4 with overlapping runs" and being positive and all that. This, unfortunately, has put a lot of young people off the game. If I had the time, and people wanted me, that's the job I'd love to see done. Now that times have changed, you see, and there are so many other things for youngsters to do, football has to dangle a bigger carrot before them. It's got to be fun – bigger goals, if you like, smaller teams – and let them play. The game as a whole must adapt, and that means breaking down the barriers.

'But after all my years in football I'm beginning to wonder if people will ever change. This is not a new subject by any means, and I well remember a famous name in the Merseyside area, Bill Roberts. He was manager of the England Schoolboys, and I ran on with the sponge. He was a headmaster in the Wirral and he once said to me, "If only we could get these sixteen boys and put them in a school which satisfied the Department of Education and Science's requirement on academic subjects but had a bias towards producing football players like the music schools ..." Well, that made sense to me then and it makes even more sense to me now. Call them schools of excellence, call them what you like. Have your hard-bitten professional there, have your more sensitive teacher who's got a feeling for the game, because that's what it's really about – we could sort them out. Yes, it's a dream probably, nothing more. But I've been to Dresden in East Germany and seen children, hand-picked for their ability at various sports, go to this sort of school and I was very impressed. I don't subscribe to their political way of life, but it makes you think.'

When people involved in professional football argue for access to younger boys, the counter-argument often is: 'Ah, but you only want the best for your own club.' The reasonable answer could be: 'And why not?' But there is widespread suspicion of the motives of professional football in this country, and the reasons are not wholly clear. Perhaps those clubs who have allowed youngsters to neglect their education have not helped. Certainly in West Germany, to give one European example, clubs have a much better reputation in this regard. Borussia Dortmund encouraged their highly promising young sweeper, Ralf Loose, to complete A-levels, several times allowing him to study in the morning before playing for the first team in the afternoon. And there was the unusual case of international goalkeeper Eike Immel, who joined Borussia from a small club at 13 after being allowed by his parents to leave the family's farm near Frankfurt, some two hundred miles away, to live with a local family in Dortmund. He left school at 14 and, while playing for Borussia's junior team, took an apprenticeship in shop management, all the while remaining under the expert guidance of the professional coaching staff. It is not uncommon for players in the Bundesliga to continue with their studies. The World Cup star Paul Breitner of Bayern Munich is perhaps the best-known example. Six of Borussia's young first team are presently at college, and even Immel is hoping to follow in their footsteps with the ready help of the club, whose enlightened attitude might be copied by a few British clubs if circumstances permitted. We prefer, say Borussia, to get players when they are young and help them with their education. It's better than buying well-known players from elsewhere – it's cheaper!

CHAPTER TEN

All the suggestions we have heard for smoothing the rocky road from schoolboy to superstar beg one question: What are the chances? Professional football's image, in Britain at least, is that of a gradually shrinking game. Crowds have been steadily decreasing and last summer several hundred footballers were put out of work. In the future, a part-time job may be the best that can be offered by some of our League clubs. But the opportunities will still be there in numbers enough to keep the dream alive in millions of young minds. The odds will still be against success, but the world of opportunity is getting wider now that careers can be made in North America and other places as well as at home. Here, despite all the forecasts of doom, many clubs will adapt and survive. Even if, for some, survival means semi-professionalism, that can still be a very rewarding life. In Scotland, for instance, the part-time players of Partick Thistle have twice in recent years been offered the chance of full-time careers with the club – and rejected it because they can earn more by combining two occupations.

There is also the beneficial effect the recession has had on some clubs, who have found they cannot afford transfer fees and adopted long-overdue youth programmes. Newcastle United, for instance, got into the headlines for signing Kevin Keegan but made an even more significant move when they ran out of money and harnessed their future to the local youngsters. Jackie Milburn, one of the club's great centre-forwards of the past, believes this could be their salvation. He recalls that after the Second World War the club had to rely on Tyneside talent and won promotion, watched by an average crowd of 56,000, before embarking on a glorious era that brought three F.A. Cup triumphs in five years. If the new generation prove half as good as Milburn's lot, the crowds will come rolling back and job opportunities should improve at St James Park. If the tendency for clubs to neglect young, home-produced players is reversed throughout the country, with coaches perhaps being given the new opportunities they seek to form a relationship with the local schools, football can only benefit.

It is heartening, too, that the kind of footballer the crowds love to see is still emerging, for all the changes in social patterns and the near-disappearance of football from many of our streets. Certainly Glenn Hoddle is an exceptional player, but he is also inspirational. And there is the case of young Trevor Steven, a product of a rugby-playing school, who became established in the Burnley team during the 1981/2 season and has skills that can only have been there at birth. The Hoddle phenomenon astonished Glenn's father, a former amateur player of some note, who could hardly believe the untutored technique displayed by his child. At the age of 8, Glenn could do almost everything he can do today. 'Except for one thing,' Glenn remembers. 'I couldn't catch the ball on the back of my neck, which was too small. It really annoyed me. I took years to perfect that trick.'

Glenn was brought up in the new town of Harlow, Essex, far from the old image of the backstreet kids learning their skills on cobbled streets, but something inside him made him want to establish the mastery of his feet over objects. He found a full-size ball too easy, and instead played keep-up with a table tennis ball, an orange, or even a marble to maintain the challenge. When people talk about Glenn lacking a little bit of determination, they should perhaps bear this in mind – if only more young players were dedicated in the way he was, the game of football would be an exciting entertainment indeed.

Skill is inevitably a subject that crops up when Glenn is discussed, but what exactly is skill? Definitions vary. Tom Saunders offers this one: 'Skill is the selection of the appropriate technique in a given situation.' He refers, of course, to the modern game, which is so fast and tight, with space at a far greater premium than in the far-off days when football was blossoming as a spectator sport. Few coaches would disagree with Tom, although it would be a pity if the occasional inappropriate technique, the flourish of arrogance, the delight of playing to the crowd, were to be neglected by the players of the future. They will have to thrill people if they want to make a living.

Football may be ever-changing, but there are certain things of which the crowds never tire. In a wonderful book about the joys of the game in boom times after the Second World War (*Barnsley: A Study in Football 1953–9*, Crowberry, 1981), Andrew Ward and Ian Alister write: 'At outside-left was the main attraction, Johnny Kelly. A winger of great individual talent would really bring in the crowds, as Stanley Matthews proved everywhere he went, and Kelly was a cheeky, effervescent entertainer. If he had a fault, it was allowing his man to recover with a view to beating him again. *The spectators seldom complained.*' The italics are mine, and I believe the professional coaches of England must bear those words in mind if they ever do achieve their ambition of greater access to schoolboy players. Otherwise not only might they disappoint some of the boys but also put at risk their own chances of eventually contributing to an improvement in the standard of the first-class game. Because at professional level football is supposed to be an entertainment and, at amateur level, a pleasure. Still, with all the risks, the chance is worth taking. We should wish the coaches well.

Encouragingly, there have been few complaints about the links that have been forged in Scotland, where many of the barriers have already been removed. In 1975 the Scottish F.A. appointed Andy Roxburgh, a former teacher and centre-forward with Partick Thistle, as the national director of coaching. He has since become involved in all levels of youth football, from the schools right up to the management of the highly successful national youth squad – the 1982 European champions. The S.F.A.'s staff coaches, most of whom work with professional clubs, have access to school-boys as young as 10 and Andy says, 'The clubs have become, if you like, our centres of excellence.' The boys, who can be signed on forms at 13, go to professional outfits such as Aberdeen, where expert tuition is given by the youth coaches Bobby Clark, a former international goalkeeper, and Lenny Taylor. Both, incidentally, are also school teachers. There have been a few of the usual doubts expressed by traditionalists among the Scottish Schools' Football Association, but the committee are firm supporters of the new system, especially now that several boys from the Scottish Schools' team have progressed to the professional youth squad. The link has been established and Andy says, 'I doubt if it will be broken now.'

Whatever happens in England, it is perhaps inevitable that managers, coaches, the directors who employ them to run the clubs, and the teachers who first spot talent in a youngster, will always argue about the best way of bringing out its full potential. It is equally certain that, whatever improvements they may make, the seeds of success can only grow from within the boy. There will always be those who work away quietly at their skills, missing out on opportunities of getting into the game for educational and other reasons, and who still come through as surely as any of the others to become international players. Our story, you remember, began with Steve Coppell, who missed an apprenticeship but got a degree – and even today prefers to clean his own boots at Manchester United because that way he knows they will be done properly: the epitome of quiet dedication. There may be disappointments to come, but Steve will survive because – like all the other career-builders we have met – he is determined to do so. They are all sportsmen, but with a burning resentment of losing because it deflects them from the pursuit of their dream. Tom Saunders, with his long experience of winners, sums it up: 'A career in football is like the Grand National. You get all those horses going round there and it's all about big hearts. There are some who have done six fences and that's enough for them, so off goes the jockey. He can't win and neither can they. It's the same with our kind of animals.'

CHAPTER ELEVEN

For Tony Cottee, the dream flowered into reality at twenty-five minutes past three on New Year's Day 1983. The seventeen-year-old West Ham fan, from an East End family steeped in soccer, made his first appearance for the Hammers, against Spurs, in front of 33,000 people at Upton Park ... and scored. He will always remember the moment: 'It was a header – I got it just right and my arms were shooting up into the air even before it hit the net. Then all hell let loose. I didn't know what to do – it was unbelievable, a tremendous, unforgettable feeling.'

West Ham went on to win the match, setting the seal on a schoolboy fantasy come true. The first inkling that Tony might be playing had come only the previous morning, when he reported for training as usual with the youth team. Mick McGiven, one of the West Ham coaches, pulled him on one side and said: 'I think you might be needed for training with the first team. You'd better go home, and report back tonight at five-thirty.' His friend Alan Dickens was told the same. Obviously, they were thrilled at being asked to train with the first team, but the idea that they might be playing against Spurs seemed remote and was to remain so until little over an hour before kick-off. Tony had been scoring goals regularly for the reserves, but he thought that, if anyone was going to be promoted, it would be Nicky Morgan, later to be transfered to Portsmouth. He didn't know that Paul Goddard, the first choice Number 8, had sprained an ankle in the match against Watford a few days earlier and was unfit for the New Year's Day match. 'Even when I found out about Paul,' he says, 'I didn't think I had a chance. I didn't think the manager would want to pitch a seventeen-year-old into a big London derby. Nicky Morgan was always the reserve striker in front of me. He was a lot older and more experienced and he had been told to report with the first team as well.

'Alan and I got there at five-thirty. In a way we were a bit disappointed to be away from our families on New Year's Eve, but the main thing we felt was that it was great to be with the first team. We had been told to take our suits to training, because we were going to stay overnight at a hotel in Epping to prepare for the match. Alan and I stayed in the same room. We had a meal of soup, steak, and gâteau in the evening and then went to bed. Even then the manager, John Lyall, did not tell us anything. Looking back I realize that was a good thing because, if he had told Alan and me we were playing, it would have put a lot of pressure on us. We might not have slept too well! Anyway, the manager told us we could sleep as late as we wanted, so Alan and I got up about ten-thirty and then we watched a bit of TV before going down into the dining-room for the pre-match meal. You could order anything you wanted. I had scrambled egg on toast. Then, still without any real feeling that we would be playing, we set off for Upton Park in a convoy of cars. I gave Alan a lift in mine. As we got closer to the ground we began to feel the atmosphere. There were people walking through the streets wearing scarves and all that. We got to the ground at a quarter to two and went to the dressing-room with the rest of the first-team squad and it was only then, just over an hour before the kick-off, that the manager called me into his little office.

'He said "Are you confident about going out there and

playing?" So I said "Yes" obviously, so he said, "Well I just want you to go out there and play your normal game. Don't feel under any pressure at all. All the lads will help you. Just go out there and do your best – and really enjoy it." Alan was called in too and he must have been as thrilled as me.

'The first thing I tried to do was to ring my Mum and Dad in Romford to let them know, but they are West Ham supporters – the whole family are – and they had already left for the ground. So when they arrived they were unaware that I was playing. My name was not even in the match programme! So it was quite a surprise for them when they heard their son's name being announced among the team changes over the loudspeakers. Finding out so late, I just had not had the chance to tell all the people I would have wanted to be there, but as it turned out there was not only my Mum and Dad there, but my brother and my two Grans.

'Everything had gone so quickly, but suddenly the thought hit me, "God, I am going out to play in front of thirty odd thousand people." I was a bit nervous. But once I actually got on to the pitch I was all right. This was the moment I had dreamed about. It was only a couple of years earlier that I had been on the terraces, watching Billy Bonds and Alan Devonshire – now I was in the same team! I tried to take it all in. But, as I say, it all happened so quickly.

'The atmosphere in the dressing-room was quite light-hearted but from half past two onwards it got more serious with everyone getting down to the business and trying to gee each other up. We did a collective warm-up, stretching muscles and so on. Everyone wished each other the best of luck. The manager made a few points to some of the players, but he is not really one for saying a lot and, as far as I was concerned, he just told me to play my normal game. He told

Alan the same. He didn't give me any tips about the Spurs defenders or anything like that.

'Running on to the pitch was a tremendous feeling, and I did my best to drink it all in before the match began. We got off to quite a good start. Although Spurs put us under pressure, we survived it pretty well and eventually the ball was played up to me down the right-hand side of the pitch. I got fouled from behind and a free kick was awarded. I just made a run into the box and watched the free kick, taken by Geoff Pike, coming over. I made a run to the near post and, as the ball went over my head, I turned around and saw Joe Gallagher jumping to head it for goal. Ray Clemence, the Spurs goalkeeper, just got a touch onto the crossbar and the ball bounced down off the underside. I just turned, instinctively, and darted in. I got my header just right, my arms were in the air and ... well, it was pandemonium. I didn't know what to do – I just ran to Paul Allen. We were winning, and I had scored! We kept control of the game. Ray Stewart scored the second goal from a penalty and I played a part in the third, which went all the way from our goalkeeper Phil Parkes to Geoff Pike, who scored. And we finished convincing winners. I was really pleased.

'I had always been confident I could play in the First Division and I thought I had done well in adapting to the style. It is obviously a lot quicker and brainier than what I had been accustomed to in reserve or youth team football. It is more one-touch – you have to react a lot quicker. I was tired towards the end, with cramp in both legs, but I had coped with the Spurs defenders and been able to hold off their challenges. There were none of the tricks I had expected from watching games on television, like shirt-pulling and all that and, as for aggravation, they didn't even talk to me until the final whistle, when they just said well done.'

As soon as he reached the dressing-room, Tony, the debut

hero, became the focus of attention from the press, radio and TV. The sponsors wanted him too – he had been voted Man of the Match and they presented him with a video game. As the reporters converged, he was interviewed for the BBC and independent radio as well as the national papers, whose reporters knew they had a 'Star is Born' fairytale to put before their readers. He was also interviewed by Brian Moore for ITV's 'The Big Match', which was to be shown later the same evening.

'It was unbelievable,' he says, 'but I just sat there and enjoyed it all. Publicity does not bother me at all because I am pretty level-headed and I feel I can deal with it. In the end, though, I just sneaked off, because I wanted to see my Mum and Dad. I signed a few autographs on my way to the car, and drove home alone. We just had the night in – my Mum and Dad, two Grans, brother and sister – and watched "The Big Match" on the TV. It was all right until the after-match interview came on! They all said how nice I looked and that, which was embarrassing. Then the TV started playing the goal all over again, from all the angles, and I got fed up of it in the end.'

Tony's father, Clive Cottee, remembers the whole family being clustered around the television set and at one stage Brian Moore saying there would be big celebrations in the Cottee household tonight. 'We were just sitting there,' Clive recalls, 'I think "emotionally drained" would be the expression. I think we had got a Chinese supper in and there might have been a couple of tins of beer open.'

A happy night was tinged with sadness, though, for as Clive explains, two much-loved members of the family were absent. The grandfathers, both ardent West Ham fans, had not lived long enough to see Tony run out in the claret and blue colours. Mrs Cottee's father had actually collapsed and died in the forecourt at Upton Park on the way into a match against West Bromwich Albion in 1980. Clive's father had died five years earlier, soon after predicting that Tony, then aged only nine, would play for the Hammers. Clive was standing next to him watching Tony in a park match at the time. 'Tony had got three or four goals and my Dad just turned to me, and said "Mark my words, I'll see him play at Upton Park." And my Dad was not the kind of man who said that sort of thing usually – when he did, everyone took notice. But there you are, he and my wife's Dad missed it when it actually happened. And of course the two Grans cried their eyes out at Upton Park during the game. They could not help it.'

At least, Tony and his Dad agree, it was fitting that the two Grans should be there. Clive says: 'We were not taking any chances. My mother is in her late seventies and actually lives up in Coventry, but I had gone up there for her birthday a couple of days earlier and I was still there when Tony rang and said he was in the squad for the New Year's Day game. So I brought her down on New Year's Eve, just in case.' Tony recalls: 'I told Dad I was only in the squad but he agreed we could not take a chance. They could not miss it for the world. And, as he said, they wouldn't be worried if I didn't play, because they love football anyway and would enjoy the game.'

Clive's brother was also there, as well as Tony's old sports master, who had flu at the time and had to take to his bed for three weeks afterwards. It was an emotional day for all concerned after a night of waiting and wondering. 'I'm glad Tony slept,' said Clive, 'because I don't think any of the rest of us did. We were all thinking, "Will he? Won't he? Course he won't! I dunno, maybe he will!" We had all seen it coming for years really. We thought in our own minds that, all things being equal, it should happen one day. But suddenly, it is about to happen and you can't believe it. I'll never forget turning to my Mum during the match and telling her, "Hey, there's another twenty-one players on the pitch!"'

There was never any doubt that Tony would become a footballer, least of all in his own mind. His father, a former amateur player, ran a club for under thirteens called Romford Royals, seven members of which went on to become apprentices at London professional clubs. But Clive was never obsessed with results and always took time to help Tony practise his skills. 'I remember he would often ask me to come over to the park and just keep knocking balls on to his left foot, or maybe I would dive in the mud at his feet if he wanted a one-on-one – that sort of thing.' By the time Clive, building up his insurance brokerage, found himself having to devote more and more time to business, Tony had progressed to a local club called Chase Cross United and that was when he was spotted by the West Ham scout Ronnie Gale. Arsenal and Crystal Palace were also interested, and Tony trained with both of them, but his love of the Hammers made it a foregone conclusion that he would pledge himself to Upton Park at fourteen, given the chance.

His favourite players included Billy Bonds, Trevor Brooking, Alan Devonshire, and above all Pop Robson, a great goal-scorer whose style is undoubtedly echoed in Tony's today. As soon as Tony left school, John Lyall asked him to become an apprentice. 'It was one of the best days of my life,' he says. 'My school work had always suffered because of football – and at last I was free to get on with the game at my favourite club. The idea never crossed my mind that I wouldn't make it. You've either got it or you haven't and I have always had a lot of confidence in myself. I have always scored goals.'

His first season at West Ham was in the youth side, which won the Southern Floodlit Junior Cup. He scored fifty-five goals. He started the 1982/3 season well and went on tour with the England youth side. All of a sudden he was in the reserves, and still the goals kept going in. And then he was in the first team. After scoring in the Spurs match he picked up another goal the following Tuesday, at home to Luton. 'It was after about twenty minutes. Sandy Clark was trying to beat a few defenders. They shut him down and I don't think he meant it but the ball came my way around the edge of the six-yard box and I just swung my left leg and luckily it went through the keeper's legs – but they all count.'

Luton won the match 3–2 with a Paul Walsh hat-trick, but Tony had little time to dwell on the disappointment because on the Friday he travelled north to face Manchester United at Old Trafford. It was his first time on the coach with the senior squad and he sat with Paul Allen because Alan Dickens was unfit for the trip. They had a meal in their hotel, the Midland, before going to sleep. Again Tony was not certain of a place in the side, because although Paul Goddard was still unavailable, there were other options open to John Lyall such as switching François Van Der Elst up front and playing an extra midfield player. But he was picked, and revelled in the Old Trafford atmosphere, watched by a crowd of over 44,000. It was also quite a kick to be up against Bryan Robson so soon after watching him play in the World Cup on television. 'I did not think I would be making such a big step up so quickly,' he says. But United won 2–0 and Tony was dropped for the next match. He returned to the side later in the season and showed that he still had the knack of goal-scoring that should keep him in the First Division limelight for years to come.

'It has been a super start,' says his father. 'But he has quite a pedigree you know. He holds the record for the Essex youth side and once scored six goals in a 7–0 victory. The record was previously held by Jimmy Greaves, then taken over by Glenn Hoddle, then Tom English of Leicester ... and then Tony. If he keeps his feet on the ground he can do as well as any of them. And I have not too many worries on that. He may be super-confident, but I don't think you will ever have a problem with the size of his hat. He grew up with good habits, and I hope like any good father I gave him that, but now his dedication and single-mindedness have taken over – and they will see him to the top.'

APPENDIX

Football as a Career – Notes for Schoolboys

Most boys at some stage or other are attracted by the thought of becoming a professional footballer. However, it must be obvious to most people that whilst football can be a profitable and most enjoyable career, there are many pitfalls. It might be helpful if some thought is given to the following points:

1. It is a fact that scouts from clubs observe many school and youth matches and it is very rare for a boy with a lot of talent to be overlooked. In other words, if you are good enough there should be no need for you to approach a club. They will contact you or your parents or your headmaster.

2. However, you can write to a club asking for a trial or asking for someone to come and see you play. You should give details of forthcoming fixtures in which you are involved and it is as well to have a recommendation from your Games master or someone like that. Obviously, you stand a better chance approaching clubs in the Third or Fourth Division of the Football League.

3. If you are outstanding, you may be offered a chance to become an 'associated schoolboy', in which case you attend the ground for coaching and training sessions. However, you can only play for the club with the written permission of your headmaster, and until the season

following your fifteenth birthday, you can only play for the club's team of associated schoolboys against schoolboy opposition. Associated schoolboy forms must be signed by yourself, your parents and your headmaster and you should seek advice from your Careers teacher and a representative of the English Schools' Football Association before any forms are signed.

4. If you become an associated schoolboy, the club has an option on your services when you leave school. You must give the club three months' notice prior to leaving school and the club must then let you know within fourteen days whether they wish to sign you as a full-time apprentice. There is an appeals procedure if there is a disagreement about the contract and you may be allowed to sign for an alternative club in some circumstances. If the club with which you were an associated schoolboy do not offer you an apprenticeship, you are free to sign for any other club.

5. Apprenticeships normally last until your eighteenth birthday. However, it is important to bear in mind that you can become a full-time professional at 17. In the circumstances, it may be in your interest to wait a year and sign as a full professional at 18, especially if you can stay on at school, or have an alternative job to go to or you are accepted for a course of Further or Higher Education. A growing number of boys are joining professional clubs after they have completed a course of Higher Education or an apprenticeship in another trade and this is by far the best course of action. As a full professional you will be able to negotiate much better terms than as an apprentice professional.

6. If you sign as an apprentice, the club will be required to train you, if desired, in an outside job, trade or profession

and/or to make adequate provision for you to continue your Further Education. At present, this normally means that you will be allowed to attend college on a part-time basis, for example, on a day-release course. Before signing your contract, you should ensure that provision is made for you to attend college for at least one full day each week and on the appropriate day for the particular course. It is obviously in your interest to continue your education and if one club will not permit this, you should be able to find another which will. If you sign as a professional, you can still arrange to be allowed to continue your education.

7. The failure rate in football is very high. The majority of associated schoolboys are not offered apprenticeships and only a minority of apprentices make a career in the game, so you can see why it is important to do as well as you can at school and to prepare for an alternative career whilst you are an apprentice or a young player.

8. In any event, professional football is a very short career, averaging less than ten years and only a tiny minority stay in the game as managers, trainers, etc., so that it is vital for players to continue to prepare for a second career throughout their time as a player.

9. The Professional Footballers' Association is the recognized Trade Union for professional footballers and all players are recommended to become members. If you are offered terms as an apprentice (or as a professional), you should contact Mr G. Taylor, Secretary, The Professional Footballers' Association, 124 Corn Exchange Buildings, Hanging Ditch, Manchester M4 3BN, before signing.

Also in Puffin Plus

Brian Glanville's
BOOK OF FOOTBALLERS

Using his incomparable worldwide knowledge of the game, Brian Glanville has compiled an alphabetical guide to great footballers, past and present, European and South American. Many contemporary stars from around the world have been included – every football lover will find this book invaluable.

MURPHY'S MOB
Michael Saunders

To save his Fourth Division Strugglers, new soccer chief Murphy takes chances – involving kids who could damage his cause. A totally contemporary story about youngsters and authority, based on the popular TV series by Brian Finch.

MURPHY & CO.
Anthony Masters

Money is still short at Dunmore United so the Junior Supporters Club – the Mob – decide to help out. But their efforts look puny beside the half a million which someone else comes up with. *Half a million?* The Mob smell a rat and decide to find out just what's going on.

THE SCARECROWS
Robert Westall

While reluctantly spending the summer at his hated stepfather's house, Simon Wood takes refuge from family pressures in an old mill house across the fields. A discarded newspaper shows that it has been empty since 1943, but somehow Simon knows that there's more to the mill than meets the eye. Someone or something is watching and waiting, but for what? When the scarecrows appear, he knows that it's only a matter of time before he is faced with a terrifying test.

THE SEVENTH RAVEN
Peter Dickinson

A modern thriller, mixing high tension and social comedy in a powerful brew. Doll, just 17, was watching the cast of children stream into the old church when she heard the gunshot. A few moments later, she and the children were the hostages of a gang of terrorists – and this year's Christmas opera had turned into a different kind of drama altogether.

MOSES BEECH
Ian Strachan

Peter was on the run from his layabout father, and Moses offered him shelter in his isolated cottage. They got on well, but for how long could Moses's unhurried way of life survive this sudden intrusion? The answer came all too quickly – and tragically.

PROVE YOURSELF A HERO
K. M. Peyton

Kidnapping is a terrifying enough experience itself, but Jonathan finds that his eventual release causes even greater problems!

TROOPER JACKSON'S STORY
Brian Thompson

It is 1914, and Sam Jackson finds himself in a crack cavalry regiment fighting Germans, forced to grow up very rapidly and cope with situations way beyond his eighteen-year-old experience. Set in the First World War, this is a moving study of that war's effect on one young man.

THE PIGMAN'S LEGACY
Paul Zindel

Consumed with guilt and grief since the death of Mr Pignati, nicknamed the Pigman, John and Lorraine determine to help another old man they find in his abandoned house. They force their way into his life, full of plans to make amends for their past mistakes, but things go wrong and they begin to wonder if the Pigman's legacy is simply too much for them to handle.

THE DEVIL ON THE ROAD
Robert Westall

John Webster took no chances with his Triumph Tiger-Cub, but he thought he played games with Chance, like tossing a coin to see which road to follow. But maybe Chance was playing games with him?

THE MOTORCYCLING BOOK
John Dyson

Buying a bike, driving safely, knowing how it works ... virtually everything an inexperienced rider needs to know about motorcycles and mopeds is brought together in this comprehensive guide. Follow its advice and you will get the best value from owning and riding a two-wheeler.

WHY DIDN'T THEY TELL THE HORSES?
Christine McKenna

Actress Christine McKenna had never been on a horse in her life, apart from an endearing donkey on the beach at the age of three. So when she landed the star role of the hunting and riding Christina in the TV serial *Flambards*, some incredible experiences were ahead of her. This is the good-natured, frequently hilarious story of one diminutive actress and her relationship with a host of horses ... some cooperative, some disdainful, and many stars in their own right.

I CAN JUMP PUDDLES
Alan Marshall

This is Alan Marshall's story of his childhood – a happy world in which, despite his crippling poliomyelitis, he plays, climbs, fights, swims, rides and laughs. His world was the Australian countryside early this century: rough-riders, bushmen, farmers and tellers of tall stories – a world all the more precious to a small crippled boy.

THE ENNEAD
Jan Mark

A vivid and compelling story about Euterpe, the third planet in a system of nine known as the Ennead, where scheming and bribery are needed to survive.

A MIDSUMMER NIGHT'S DEATH
K. M. Peyton

When the body of the unpopular English master, Mr Robinson, was taken from the river, Jonathan didn't feel very involved in the tragedy. But it was disturbing to realize that another master had lied to the police about not seeing Robinson on the evening before his death. And soon Jonathan was beginning to doubt whether the coroner's verdict of suicide had been the right one. An absorbing thriller, by the author of *Flambards*.